650.1   Males, Carolyn
MAL

Life after high
school

10541

$10.29

DATE			

© THE BAKER & TAYLOR CO.

LIFE AFTER
HIGH SCHOOL

A CAREER
PLANNING GUIDE

LIFE AFTER HIGH SCHOOL

A CAREER PLANNING GUIDE

by Carolyn Males
and Roberta Feigen

Julian Messner New York

Published by Julian Messner,
A Division of Simon & Schuster, Inc.
Simon & Schuster Building
Rockefeller Center
1230 Avenue of the Americas
New York, New York 10020

JULIAN MESSNER and colophon are
trademarks of Simon & Schuster, Inc.

10 9 8 7 6 5 4 3 2

Manufactured in the United States of America
Designed by Elizabeth Fox

Library of Congress Cataloguing in Publication Data

Males, Carolyn.
    LIFE AFTER HIGH SCHOOL: A Career Planning Guide
    Bibliography: p.
    Includes index.
    Summary: Techniques for planning a career and
finding a job, with advice in self analysis of skills
and goals, interviewing, making resumes and applications,
and building confidence.
    1. Vocational guidance—Juvenile literature.
2. Job hunting—Juvenile literature. 3. Employment
interviewing—Juvenile literature. [1. Vocational
guidance. 2. Job hunting. 3. Employment interviewing]
I. Feigen, Roberta. Title.
HF5381.2.M34   1986   331.7′023   85-43383

ISBN: 0-671-54664-3

Acknowledgments

We would like to thank the pioneers of career counseling—Richard N. Bolles, John Holland, and John Crystal, and all the other contributors to the field whose studies, theories, and techniques have provided the basis for career counseling today. Over the years their ideas have guided us in counseling many clients.

Special thanks to Jerry Feigen and the Small Business Administration for providing us with information for Chapter Five, Beginning Your Own Business.

Thanks, too, to the many clients, students, and workshop participants who contributed ideas and shared their problems and solutions with us. We would also like to thank the other career counselors, workshop leaders, trainers, and teachers who have shared their expertise with us.

We would especially like to thank our children, Lisa and Philip Feigen and Richard Males, for being an inspiration and impetus for writing this book and for helping make this book relevant to young people. We'd like to thank our husbands, Jerry Feigen and Dick Males, for all their love and support. Finally, we would like to thank our agent, Linda Hayes, for her faith in us and our editor, Jane Steltenpohl, for her help in guiding this book to completion.

CONTENTS

work. Making your own job leads. Preparing for job interviews. Doing your homework. Following up. Dealing with rejection.

INTRODUCTION: Planning For Your Future

How often have you been asked, "What are you going to do when you finish school?" And how many times have you mumbled, "I don't know," or found yourself stammering, turning red, shifting from foot to foot, and shrugging. Maybe you're the wisecracking type who answers, "Oh, I'm planning to be a beachcomber on the moon."

Perhaps you're worrying about how you'll ever decide what to do. You may have given your future some thought, but you may still find yourself standing at the crossroads of indecision, scratching your head. Which way should you go?

To add to all the confusion, technology is rapidly revolutionizing the world, and new jobs seem to pop up each day. Everyone knows what a doctor or a supermarket clerk does; you see people working in these occupations all the time. But what about all the new jobs in robotics, computers, biogenetics, ocean-

1

ography, and telecommunications? What do people who work in these areas do? Career fields are changing every day as new jobs develop and old ones disappear. For example, if you were looking to make some extra money this summer as a mail clerk in a large corporation, you may be surprised. Robots have taken over the job of mail delivery in some large corporations and in some departments of the federal government. However, these companies will need technicians to repair and maintain their robots.

What kinds of jobs will be available when you enter the job market? What salaries will employers pay? What training or education will you need? Your head is probably swimming with questions. How can you possibly decide now what you're going to do with the rest of your life?

Maybe you're not ready to plan it all today. But if you are at a crossroads—trying to make up your mind whether to go to college, take additional courses, or find a job—you probably need to start planning. This book can show you how to map out a career plan and how to make decisions. You can use this method over and over again at each decision point in your life. You'll find that your career path can be smooth, rocky, or full of potholes, depending upon the route you choose. It can be a roller-coaster road of highs and lows or as straight as a newly paved highway. The trick is to make the best choices and avoid stumbling in potholes and getting lost in dead ends along the way.

This self-help planning guide is designed to take some of the scariness out of making career choices by helping you discover what you are good at doing and by showing you a way to explore different occupations. In addition, you will learn how to prepare a resume, line up job interviews, build your confidence, and present yourself effectively on a job interview.

GETTING STARTED

You are about to embark upon a journey of self-discovery where you will explore what you like to do, what your talents and strengths are, and what's important to you. Along the way you'll be gathering information about yourself and the world of work. You will record your discoveries in a career journal. You can use a loose-leaf or spiral-bound notebook for your journal. Keep this notebook just for your career planning. When you've completed all the exercises from this book and recorded them in your journal, you'll have a complete career plan to guide you through the coming years.

Take a few minutes to daydream. First read through the questions below. Then close your eyes and pretend you're in a time machine traveling to a day ten years from now. Stop the machine and try to picture what a typical day ten years into the future might look like. What are you doing? What do you look like? Now open your eyes. Label the first page of your notebook "My Future Day" and write down your answers.

■ What did you look like? What kind of clothes were you wearing?

- How were you traveling about? Car, train, bus, plane?
- What kind of place did you go to?
- What kind of work or activities were you doing?

Now you have a vision of what you might want to do. Let's go on and begin planning.

1
TAKING
THE FIRST
STEP

Now that you've taken a trip in our time machine ten years into the future, step into the machine once again and this time go back over the past few years of your life. What are some of the activities you've enjoyed doing? What do you like to do now—read, bake, jog, surf, bike, play basketball, train your pet, write poetry, or play computer games?

ACTIVITIES: WHAT HAVE YOU BEEN DOING?

Take out your career journal and write "Activities I Enjoy" across the top of a page. Then start compiling a list of everything you enjoy doing. Don't worry about how big or small the activity is. Go ahead and list "planting a few flowers around a tree," along with "planting an entire vegetable garden." You may include activities from when you were a small child as well as those you've taken part in recently. Here's the list that Bob made.

ACTIVITIES I ENJOY

1. taking pictures
2. watching football games
3. talking to my friends
4. hiking
5. reading sports biographies
6. writing stories

DISCOVERING SKILLS: WHAT CAN YOU DO?

Every activity requires skills. A skill is an ability, something you've learned to do well and have done over and over again. And everyone, including you, has skills. Bob loves taking photographs, particularly action sports shots. For the past few years, he's been taking pictures of the football team for the school newspaper and yearbook. He always thought of this activity as a hobby, something he did for fun. He never realized that he'd picked up a lot of skills while he was out snapping shots of guys in padded shoulders and helmets. His school counselor pointed out that photography requires artistic skills as well as an understanding of football. On the activity page of his career journal, Bob added a column called "Skills I Used" and in it wrote down the skills he had used in each activity.

ACTIVITIES I ENJOY	SKILLS I USED
1. taking pictures	photography, artistic ability
2. watching Redskins games	observation, planning strategies
3. talking to my friends	social skills, communication, listening
4. hiking	athletic ability
5. reading sports biographies	reading, learning
6. writing stories	creativity, writing, and editing skills

Now go over the activities you've written down on your "Activities I Enjoy" page. Jot down the skills you used in each activity, just as Bob did.

Over the years, you've taken part in many activities and developed many skills—more than you probably remember or give yourself credit for. To help you become aware of the many skills you use, or would like to use, look at the Occupational Skills chart that follows. This chart lists many different kinds of skills. These skills are broken down into occupational categories.

Read the chart. Then turn to a new page in your notebook; title it "My Skills." Using the chart as a guide, copy down all the skills you have enjoyed using. Be sure to include the ones you've already noted on your "Activities I Enjoy" page. Then write down some skills you may want to develop. Circle these skills and think about some ways you can develop them. Is there a new activity or hobby you could try? Some courses you could take? Could you take a volunteer or paid job where you'd learn that skill?

For example, Aaron had been a member of his local Explorer's Post law enforcement club. He had learned much about law enforcement, patrolling and emergency responding (all Protective skills) in his work with the post, so he wrote those skills down in his notebook. When he reread the list of Protective skills, he realized he also wanted to learn how to investigate. So he added "investigating" to his own skills list and circled it. In his future activities with the Explorer Post, he would plan to learn this new skill.

OCCUPATIONAL SKILLS CHART

ARTISTIC	SCIENTIFIC
inventive	analyzing
imaginative	decision-making
	detecting
decorating	diagnosing
designing	evaluating
	experimenting
editing	information gathering
interviewing	investigating
storytelling	mathematical
writing	measuring
	observing
crafting	organizing
drawing	problem-solving
painting	researching
photography	testing
sculpting	
acting	
composing	
dancing	
musical	
performing	
singing	
teaching	

PLANTS AND ANIMALS

farming
gardening
groundskeeping
    (lawnmowing, etc.)
landscaping

animal training
caring for animals

fishing
hunting

PROTECTIVE

emergency responding
enforcing law, regulations
firefighting
guarding
investigating
patrolling
securing

driving

MECHANICAL

adjusting
building
drafting
operating equipment
reading blueprints
reading patterns
recording sounds
repairing
testing
trouble-shooting
using tools
woodworking

cooking (creative)
sewing/tailoring

calculating

INDUSTRIAL

assembling
estimating
inspecting
laboring (general)
packing
printing
reading blueprints,
patterns
soldering
sorting
welding
wire wrapping

cleaning (rugs,
    upholstery)
cooking (general)
sewing (piecework)

MECHANICAL cont.

driving
navigating
piloting

cleaning (janitorial or
domestic)

INDUSTRIAL cont.

lifting
moving
operating machinery
using tools

BUSINESS DETAIL

accounting
bookkeeping
budgeting
checking
computing
coordinating information
counting
data entry
data processing
filing
numerical
operating business
machines
organizing
typing

SELLING

advertising
communicating
demonstrating
negotiating
persuading
promoting
speaking

ACCOMMODATING

driving
guiding

helping
hosting

HUMANITARIAN

communicating
counseling
guiding
listening
negotiating

ACCOMMODATING cont.

listening
serving

applying makeup
hairstyling
haircutting
manicuring

HUMANITARIAN cont.

nursing
speaking
teaching
training
understanding

LEADING-INFLUENCING (VERBAL SKILLS)

advising
coordinating
decision-making
designing programs
influencing
initiating
interviewing
managing
motivating
negotiating
organizing
performing
persuading
planning
problem-solving
risk-taking
running meetings
selling
supervising
time management
trouble-shooting

LEADING-INFLUENCING (NUMERICAL SKILLS)

budgeting
financial
fund-raising
mathematical
negotiating

PHYSICAL
PERFORMING

coaching
instructing

competing
demonstrating
performing

game skills
gymnastics
riding
running
skiing
swimming

JOB POSSIBILITIES: CLUES TO YOUR FUTURE

How can your activities and skills help you decide on a career or find a job that's right for you? Can Bob's shutterbug hobby lead to a job? Taking stock of the kinds of skills you have can help you move on, opening up career or job possibilities you've probably never thought about. To help you discover some of these possibilities, turn to the next page in your career journal and label it "Using My Skills." Answer each of the following questions in a complete sentence.

1. Under which two categories on the Occupational Skills Chart did most of the skills you used or want to use fall? Were most of your skills artistic? Leadership? Mechanical? (Bob wrote, "Most of my skills were artistic and physical performing.)

2. Do you like using your skills indoors or outdoors? Or both?

3. Do you like working by yourself? In a large group? A small group? With a partner?

4. Do you like working with data (information or statistics), people (or animals), or things (machines, books, tools)? You may have two answers to this question. For example, Bob likes working with people *and* things. He likes using a camera and taking pictures of people.

OCCUPATIONAL INTERESTS

Look over the Guide to Occupations on the next few pages. Pay particular attention to the jobs listed under your two main skill areas. Read the description next to each of these areas and see if it matches your interests. For example, suppose you have strong math skills. Read the description under Business Detail and under Leading-Influencing. Which jobs interest you more? If you like the idea of an office job with specific tasks, you might consider jobs like bookkeeper or tax preparer listed under Business Detail. However, if you prefer jobs that allow you to influence people as well as use your numerical ability, you might check out "mathematical" jobs like accountant, financial analyst, or economist listed under the Leading-Influencing category. (These categories of jobs are based on the *Guide for Occupational Exploration,* also called the G.O.E., which you will learn about in Chapter Three.)

Now on a new page in your journal, write down some of the jobs you see that might interest you. Label that page "Occupational Interests." There may be some jobs you've never heard of and you may want to investigate these further when you get to Chapter Three. Add any additional job interests that come to mind. Don't be afraid to consider jobs that you don't have all the necessary skills for now. You can always acquire those skills later.

GUIDE TO OCCUPATIONS

ARTISTIC

(interest in the creative expression of ideas or feelings)

critic
editor
editorial writer
film editor
lyricist
newspaper reporter
playwright
poet
screenwriter
writer

artist
audio-visual producer
cartoonist
designer
fashion artist
floral designer
graphic artist
illustrator
interior designer
photographer
photojournalist
sculptor
set designer
arts teacher

dancer
choreographer
dance instructor

art conservator
jeweler
model maker
sign painter
silversmith
taxidermist

model
modeling instructor

SCIENTIFIC

(interest in discovering, collecting, and analyzing information about the natural world and applying scientific research findings to problems in medicine, the life sciences, and the natural sciences)

astronomer
chemist
computer applications
    engineer
environmental analyst
geographer
geologist
mathematician
meteorologist
physicist

animal scientist
anthropologist
biochemist
biologist
biomedical engineer
botanist

SCIENTIFIC cont.

dietician
food technologist
geneticist
soil conservationist
zoologist

chiropractor
dentist
doctor
psychiatrist

radiologist
speech pathologist
surgeon
veterinarian

color specialist
embalmer
film laboratory technician
food tester
lab technician
pharmacist

PLANTS AND ANIMALS

(interest in working with plants and animals,
usually outdoors)

animal breeder
beekeeper
farmer
forester
horticulturalist
landscaper
rancher
tree surgeon
wildlife agent

animal caretaker

animal trainer
farm laborer
fisher
forest firefighter
groundskeeper
logger

PROTECTIVE

(an interest in using authority to protect people and property)

corrections officer
detective
fire marshal
investigator
police officer
security guard
special agent

lifeguard
park ranger
ski patroller

MECHANICAL

(applying or planning to apply mechanical principles to practical situations by use of machine or hand tools)

aeronautical engineer
chemical engineer
electronics engineer
industrial engineer
landscape architect
laser technician
manufacturing engineer
marine engineer

mechanical engineer
tool designer
nuclear engineer
petroleum engineer

construction supervisor
maintenance supervisor

MECHANICAL cont.

estimator
drafter
land surveyor

air traffic controller
navigator
transmitter operator
(radio or television)

boat captain
flying instructor
pilot
shipmate
test pilot

bricklayer
mason
stonecutter

boat builder
carpenter
house builder

plumber
pipe fitter
paperhanger

aircraft mechanic
dental lab technician
electrician
sound technician

auto body repairer or
customizer
auto mechanic
sheet metal worker

optician

gunsmith
tool grinder

cabinetmaker
furniture finisher

air conditioning mechanic
farm equipment
mechanic
locksmith

appliance repairer

biomedical technician
camera repairer
electromechanical
technician

instrument maker
instrument repairer

offset printing press
operator

dishwasher

MECHANICAL cont.

gem cutter

bookbinder
dressmaker
shoemaker
tailor
upholsterer

chef, cook
food products tester

cake decorator

heavy equipment
  operator
miner
oil well driller

chimney sweep
housecleaner
janitor

INDUSTRIAL

(interest in using skill and knowledge of
machines to perform complex activities)

industrial supervisor
laboratory supervisor

assembler
dry cleaner
food production worker
glass cutter
laborer
machine operator
meatpacker
packer

printing press operator
rug cleaner
sewing machine operator
welder

estimator
inspector
quality control inspector
sorter
tester

BUSINESS DETAIL

(an interest in organized, clearly defined activities requiring attention to details, primarily in an office setting)

administrative assistant
cashier
clerk, insurance
court clerk
driver's license examiner
financial aid counselor
office manager
secretary

billing clerk
bookkeeper
credit analyst
tax preparer

ticket agent
teller

dispatcher
fire lookout

information clerk
loan officer
survey worker
switchboard operator
telephone operator

mail carrier

proofreader

computer operator
keypunch operator
typist

file clerk
library page

SELLING

(an interest in bringing others to a particular point of view by personal persuasion, using sales and promotion techniques)

SELLING cont.

auctioneer
buyer
demonstrator
real estate agent
sales representative

technical salesperson
telephone solicitor
travel agent
wedding consultant

ACCOMMODATING

(an interest in catering to the needs of others, usually on a one-to-one basis)

camp counselor
convention planner
guide
recreation leader

flight attendant
passenger service
    representative

barber
cosmetologist
hairstylist
manicurist

bus driver
chauffeur
driving instructor
taxi driver

car wash attendant
game attendant
parking lot attendant

customer service clerk

bartender
host, hostess
waiter, waitress

porter
usher

wardrobe supervisor

HUMANITARIAN

(an interest in helping others with their mental, social, physical or vocational needs)

caseworker
clergyman, clergywoman
counselor
parole officer
psychiatrist
psychiatric aide
psychologist
social worker
teacher

art therapist
industrial therapist
occupational therapist
recreational therapist
nurse
physical therapist
physician's assistant

ambulance attendant

dental hygienist
emergency medical
    technician

child care worker
foster parent
tutor

LEADING-INFLUENCING

(an interest in leading and influencing others by using high level verbal or numerical abilities)

computer programmer
financial analyst
statistician
systems analyst

home economist
homemaker
librarian
media specialist
teacher

anthropologist
economist
historian
linguist
occupational analyst
psychologist
sociologist
urban planner

LEADING-INFLUENCING cont.

district attorney
judge
lawyer
paralegal assistant
tax attorney

business manager
personnel manager
station manager

accountant
auditor
financial analyst
mathematician
stockbroker

administrator, human
    services

broadcaster
news editor

reporter
translator

fund-raiser
lobbyist
promoter
public relations
    representative

revenue officer
safety inspector
customs inspector

apartment manager
club manager
innkeeper

contracts officer
leasing agent
literary agent

PHYSICAL PERFORMING

(interest in physical activities before an audience)

athlete
coach
sports instructor

umpire

racing driver

PHYSICAL
PERFORMING cont.

equestrian	juggler
jockey	
rodeo performer	stunt performer
acrobat	

You've just taken the first step in your career plan—discovering your skills and some career or job possibilities. But it's difficult to make a career choice before you've made some decisions about how you want to lead your life and what you want to accomplish. Let's move on to set some priorities about life and work.

2
DECIDING
WHAT'S
IMPORTANT
TO YOU

Before you get down to the business of actually choosing a career, it's helpful to know what your priorities in life are—what's important to you. You already know some of your skills and have some career or occupational possibilities written down in your journal. But how does this information help you decide what kind of life you want to lead? For example, suppose you're a fine dancer and you want to earn enough money to own a fancy car, buy tapes and records, and rent a roomy apartment. Unless you become a Baryshnikov or a Margot Fonteyn overnight, you've got a lot of hard work ahead of you with little money coming in. The question, then, is which is more important to you, becoming a dancer or making a good salary?

There is no right or wrong answer. Your decision will be based on what you value most highly. If comfort and money are most important to you, you may want to look at your other skills and see how you can use them in the job market. Maybe you can take your business and artistic skills and work in advertising or public relations. One graduate balanced her financial needs with her dance ambitions by working for an advertising agency during the day and dancing in dinner theater shows during the evening.

In other words, the jobs you hold will affect the way you live your life. If you decide to be an obstetrician, be prepared to have your sleep interrupted in the middle of the night by phone calls summoning you to deliver babies. However, you will satisfy your need to help other people and will probably earn a good income at the same time. If you're a clotheshorse and you choose telephone line-work as your career goal, you'll have to save your trendy wardrobe for leisure time. However, you will get to work outdoors and use your mechanical skills.

By selecting your priorities, you'll be better able to decide what's important to you in choosing a career. Take a few minutes to do the following exercises. Keep in mind that there are no right or wrong answers. Because we're all different, we have different values. You may like working with people whereas your friend may prefer working alone. The priorities you hold make you uniquely you.

LIFE PRIORITIES

Let's climb into the time machine once again and zoom into the future. What do you see there? What are your top priorities? Look at the Life Qualities list below. Which of these qualities do you value most? Now open up your career journal, write "My Life Priorities" at the top of a fresh page, and number from one to sixteen. If "happiness" is most important to you, list that in the number one spot. If "wealth" is next in importance, put it in the number two spot, and so on until you've completed your list. (*Hint:* If you get stuck after the first few, think about what's least important to you, put it on line sixteen, and work backwards.)

LIFE QUALITIES

Friendship—Forming and maintaining close personal relationships
Leadership—Influencing and directing others
Prestige—Being recognized and appreciated
Health—Being well
Wealth—Making a lot of money
Security—Being safe and holding a stable job
Independence—Having freedom of thought and action
Self-respect—Having integrity
Power—Directing or influencing others
Adventure—Living an exciting life
Happiness—Enjoying life
Family—Sharing affection with family
Knowledge—Having expertise or wisdom
Self-realization—Reaching your own potential
Aesthetics—Appreciating artistic beauty
Service—Helping others

Take a look at your top five priorities and circle them. These are the qualities you'll most want to consider in planning for your future.

WORK PRIORITIES

Now zero in on a perfect workday in the future. What activities would be important to you? Do you see yourself working with people? With data, statistics, and research materials? With machinery, cars, instruments, computers, and robots? Do you see yourself doing similar tasks over and over again or performing a variety of activities each day?

The list below contains fifteen work qualities. On the next page of your journal, write "Work Priorities" across the top and begin by putting the most important work quality on the first line, the second on the next, and so on until you get to fifteen. If you're stuck, once again you might want to begin by picking out the least important and going backwards. Remember these are qualities you value in a job.

WORK QUALITIES

Variety—Performing different activities
Teamwork—Working with others
Recognition—Being known and recognized
   by others
Working Alone—Doing things by myself
Creativity—Thinking up a new idea or
   products; having imagination
Making money—Having a high income
Independence—Controlling your own
   activities
Aesthetics—Appreciating beauty
Leadership—Influencing others
Productivity—Doing useful work or making a
   useful product

Orderliness—Doing routine, predictable
  tasks
Adventure—Doing exciting and new things
Service—Working to help others
Security—Having a stable position
Challenge—Being motivated and taking risks

Circle your top five priorities. These are qualities to keep in mind when you start looking at different careers.

Why Set Priorities?

- *You can find out what you believe in and what's important to you.*
- *You can make better choices.* For example, if you like writing and you prefer working by yourself, technical writing might be a better career choice than newspaper reporting where you have to interview lots of people.
- *You can look for alternatives.* If you really want to use your talent as a guitarist but want to keep regular nine-to-five workday hours, you can look for jobs that don't spill over into the wee hours of the morning—jobs like music teacher or salesperson in a music store rather than musician in a band.
- *You can focus on what you want to do.* Knowing that you like working with data rather than with people will help you focus on careers that fit this priority. For example, if your interest is medicine, you may choose to do medical research rather than practice as a doctor.

Now that you've discovered some of your skills and priorities, you're ready to set some goals.

GOAL SETTING

Goals are steps to making your dreams come true. Picturing what you want is the first step to achieving a goal. First you must see a goal in your mind and then think of ways to accomplish it. Jason wants to own his own ice cream shop someday. He envisions himself behind the counter of Jason's Ice Cream Parlor, creating skyscraper sundaes and ringing up sales. What can Jason do to make this dream a reality? Here's what he did.

MY LONG-RANGE GOAL: TO OWN MY OWN ICE CREAM SHOP.

Steps to achieving my goal:

1. Work in an ice cream store.
2. Take business courses.
3. Start saving money.
4. Read up on the ice cream business.
5. Talk to ice cream store owners.
6. Find out how to borrow money.
7. Taste different brands and flavors of ice cream (the good but fattening part).

These are some short-term steps Jason can take to meet this long-range goal.

Long-Range Goals

What are your long-range goals? What do you want to accomplish during your life? Sometimes it's hard to picture yourself far in the future. That's okay. The future's always a bit fuzzy and unsure. To make answering these questions easier, pretend you're an author.

If you were writing your autobiography and had to describe the next ten years of your life, what would you like to say? Maybe you'd like to go away to college, play in a racquetball tournament, write poetry, climb a mountain, learn to play the trumpet, get married, start your own business, travel to a foreign country, be self-supporting—anything you want to accomplish counts as a goal.

1. Take out your journal and label a new page "Long-Range Goals."
2. Write down some things you would like to accomplish over the next ten years. Think about this question in terms of *family, friends, job, finances, hobbies, education,* and *personal development.*
3. Put down as many goals as you can think of, placing each goal on a separate line. Write quickly and don't stop to judge what you're writing.
4. When you're done with your list, go back and circle the three most important goals on your list.

Medium-Range Goals

Now think in smaller steps. Where would you like to be three or four years from now? This is probably a little easier to visualize. After all, you probably have some idea of whether you'll be in school or out on the job. Take three minutes to answer this question on a new page in your notebook titled "Medium-Range Goals." Don't forget to think about *family, friends, job, finances, hobbies, education,* and *personal development.* When you're finished, once again circle the three most important goals.

Short-Range Goals

What would you like to accomplish in the next six months? When you set your short-range (six-month) goals, you're really zeroing in on what you want to accomplish now. As you answer this question, once again remember to think about *family, friends, job, finances, hobbies, education,* and *personal development.* On a notebook page labeled "Six-Month Goals," jot down your ideas. When you're done, once again go back and circle your most important three goals.

GETTING THERE: TAKING STEPS TOWARD YOUR GOALS

Now that you know some goals you'd like to accomplish, how do you attain them? Pick one of your favorite occupational goals from one of the three lists. Then begin jotting down in your journal the steps you could take to get there. It's easier to get what you want if you break your goal down into smaller steps. For instance, Donna, a high school freshman, wants to be a beautician. What steps could she take to get there? Here's what she wrote:

GOAL: TO BE A BEAUTICIAN

STEPS TO TAKE:

1. September   Get information at library.
2. October   Check to see what educational requirements are.
3. November   Talk to counselor at vocational high school.
4. Christmas vacation   Talk to beauticians at local beauty shops.

Donna tries to do one of these steps each month so that by the middle of the school year she'll have a pretty good idea of what a job as a beautician is like and what she has to do if she wants to become one.

Write your goal across the top of a new page in your journal just as Donna did. List "Steps to Take" to reach your goal. Then go back and assign a date for completing each step, as Donna did.

This exercise probably didn't take a lot of time. In less than an hour, you've started to plan for the next ten years. Whenever you set a goal, try listing steps you can take to accomplish it. If you remember to keep taking a few minutes to plan as you go along in life, you'll probably achieve many of your goals.

3
RESEARCHING
CAREERS

Can you imagine yourself going off to work each day for thirty or forty years? Well, that's how long the average person works in a lifetime. That's a big chunk of your life, so it's worth taking time now to explore the more than twenty thousand different kinds of jobs available. You might get dizzy just thinking about all the possibilities. How can you find the right career for you?

Don't despair. You don't have to make a decision now. This is a time for exploring and researching career options—careers you've already listed on your "Occupational Interest" page and those you haven't even begun to think about. How, then, do you learn about all those jobs out there?

Begin your exploration at the local library. Here you'll discover books, magazines, and pamphlets about the world of work. You might start by talking with the reference librarian to see if your library has a career section, or you might look in the card or computer catalog under the subject heading "Vocational guidance." Also, thumb through some of the publications listed below.

LIBRARY RESOURCES

RESOURCE

WHERE TO FIND IT

OCCUPATIONAL OUTLOOK HANDBOOK (O.O.H.)
An encyclopedia of job information published by the U.S. Department of Labor.

Reference section of public libraries, school career centers or guidance offices, community colleges, and college libraries.

DICTIONARY OF OCCUPATIONAL TITLES (D.O.T.)
A dictionary of jobs put out by the U.S. Department of Labor. The most comprehensive sourcebook for up-to-date occupational information on job duties and descriptions.

Same as above.

GUIDE FOR OCCUPATIONAL EXPLORATION (G.O.E.)
A guide with data on skills, aptitudes, interests, and training needed for occupational groups. Gives specific jobs and D.O.T. numbers.

Same as above.

YELLOW PAGES (telephone directory).

Library and home.

CAREER WORLD
A magazine for high school students about careers and jobs.

School career centers and libraries.

HOW TO USE IT

KINDS OF INFORMATION

Table of contents lists 27 job categories. Pick categories that most interest you. Read them for specific information about jobs.

Tells about career areas. Describes work, skills required, number employed in field, outlook for future. Lists salaries, related jobs, sources of information.

Find D.O.T. numbers listed next to each job in O.O.H. and G.O.E. Look up those numbers in the D.O.T. Look at related jobs in that numerical category. Alphabetical index in back of book.

Gives ideas about jobs, including little known occupations. Lists titles and job descriptions for more than 20,000 occupations.

Table of contents lists 12 major occupational areas. Look under occupational areas to find specific jobs and information about them.

For each job group, explains the kind of work done, skills and abilities and training needed. Helps evaluate your interest in these areas. Tells how to prepare for each type of work.

Look at categories of services (usually listed in front of book) for ideas about different careers.

Gives ideas about occupations available in local area.

Thumb through for articles about careers, for job-finding tips, and job ideas.

Contains information about new careers and helpful hints on career planning and job finding.

RESOURCE	WHERE TO FIND IT
CAREER AND VOCATIONAL BOOKS AND MAGAZINES Deal with specific trades and professions (for example: GUITAR WORLD, WOMEN'S WEAR DAILY, VENTURE, INC.)	In vocational guidance section and in periodical section of library.
WANT ADS Classified section of newspapers.	In newspapers at home and in libraries.
BIOGRAPHIES AND AUTOBIOGRAPHIES OF PEOPLE IN CAREER FIELDS; VOCATIONAL BIOGRAPHIES (broadcast journalist—Dan Rather; ball player—Jackie Robinson; singer-actress —Lena Horne)	Libraries and book stores.

## HOW TO USE IT	## KINDS OF INFORMATION
Choose books and magazines on careers you're interested in. Look through them to get ideas. (Books written within the past five years will give most up-to-date information.)	Descriptions of jobs, how people do them. Stories about people working in their field. Information on salary expectations and job openings. Current information in magazines and newspapers.
Scan ads. Discover what job skills are required and what salaries are offered.	Includes skills needed, salaries and benefits offered for various types of jobs. Gives an idea of number of job openings in a particular field in your local area.
Read them for a personal view of a career field.	Offers inside information about a career person's life-style, goals, struggles, and triumphs.

BEGINNING YOUR SEARCH

Here's a way to organize your library research:

1. Take your career journal with you to the library reference section. Get a copy of the *Occupational Outlook Handbook* (O.O.H.) and look through the table of contents. Pick out and read about three areas that you're interested in. Choose broad career areas like "mechanics & repairers" or "service occupations." While you're reading, open your notebook to a clean page and jot down the jobs that appeal to you. Label this page "Jobs to Explore." Also write down the *Dictionary of Occupational Titles* (D.O.T.) number listed next to the job title.

2. Now go to the D.O.T. Look up these job titles by their numbers and read the job description for each one. Remember to look at other jobs listed with similar numerical classifications. This will clue you in to related jobs. You can also look up specific jobs in the Alphabetical Index of Occupational Titles in the back of the D.O.T.

3. Another book to explore is the GUIDE FOR OCCUPATIONAL EXPLORATION (G.O.E.). Here you can find out about requirements for specific jobs. First, look up a job you're interested in in the index and find its job category number (note: these are not the same as D.O.T.

numbers). Then turn to the section where your job is discussed and read about skills and education you'll need and the kinds of things you'll do in these jobs. For example, if you're interested in becoming a biochemist, look up "Biochemist" in the index, note its number (02.02.03), then turn to the 02.02 section (Scientific: Life Sciences) in the G.O.E. where you'll learn about biochemistry and other related jobs.

4. As you look up each job you're really interested in, write the job title on the top of a page in your journal—for instance, "airline pilot." Then answer the following questions, using information from the O.O.H., the D.O.T., and the G.O.E. (*Hint:* Read through these questions. Before you answer them, look ahead to Annie's journal entry and see how she set up her page.)

OCCUPATIONAL INFORMATION

OCCUPATION.
D.O.T. NUMBER.

What does a person with this job title do?
What kinds of skills does he or she need?
How much education is required?
What is the job outlook for the future?
What is the salary range?
Related occupations:
Skills to develop:
Experience or training needed:

To answer the last two questions, go back to your "My Skills" exercise in your journal and see how the skills you have match up with those you will need to do these jobs. List any new skills you may have to develop or any experience or training you might need to work in these fields.

Annie's Page

Annie is a high school senior whose feet are off the ground and whose heart is in the sky. For her seventeenth birthday, her parents gave her flying lessons. Now Annie thinks she might want to be an airline pilot. She's gone to the library and paged through the G.O.E., O.O.H., and D.O.T. to gather information, copying only the most important facts. Here's what Annie wrote:

OCCUPATIONAL INFORMATION

OCCUPATION: AIRLINE PILOT   D.O.T. NUMBER:
                                                     196.263-014

What does a person with this job title do? (found in D.O.T.)

> Pilots airplane to transport passengers, mail or freight, or for other commercial purposes; reviews ship's papers to ascertain factors, such as load weight, fuel supply, weather conditions and flight route and schedule. Orders changes in fuel supply, load, route, or schedule to ensure safety of flight.

What kinds of skills does he or she need? (found in D.O.T.)

> Reads gauges to verify that oil, hydraulic fluid, fuel quantities, and cabin pressure are at prescribed levels prior to starting engines. Sets brakes and accelerates engines. . . . Contacts control tower by radio to obtain takeoff clearance and instructions. Releases brakes and moves throttles for takeoff. Pilots airplane to destination. Logs information such as time in flight, altitude flown and fuel consumed.

How much education is required? (found in D.O.T., G.O.E., and O.O.H.)

- Must hold a commercial pilot's certificate issued by the Federal Aviation Administration. To qualify for this license must be 18 years old; have at least 250 hours of flight experience, pass a strict health examination, have 20/20 vision (with or without glasses), good hearing and no physical handicaps that could impair performance.
- Must pass written test on principles of safe flight, navigation techniques and FAA regulations. Must also demonstrate flying ability to FAA.
- Must attend military or civilian flying schools.
- Must be a high school graduate. Most airlines prefer two years of college and some prefer college graduates.

What is the job outlook for the future? (found in
O.O.H. under "Transportation Occupations")

Jobs will increase at an average rate in
1980s. Keen competition for openings
because number of qualified pilots is
expected to exceed openings. But will be an
increase in airline traffic so more airline pilots
needed in long run. Employment of pilots
sensitive to swings in economy.

What is the salary range? (found in O.O.H.)

Average 1980 salary $67,000 a year.
Starting salaries for flight engineer average
$14,400 per year. Senior captains on largest
aircraft earn as much as $110,000 a year.
Pilots not working for major airlines earn
lower salaries.

Related occupations (found in O.O.H., D.O.T., and
G.O.E.)

Helicopter pilot, air traffic controller and
dispatcher, flight instructor

Skills to develop (found in G.O.E. under "Air and
Vehicle Operation")

Piloting and navigating; knowing about
load weight, fuel supply, weather conditions,
flight routes; reacting quickly in emergencies;
supervising crews

Experience and training needed

More lessons, ground school, earn
license, put in more flying time

When Annie finished her section on airline pilot, she set up and filled out pages for two of her other career interests—physical education teacher and sports store owner. Also, whenever she can, Annie reads books on pilots and sports to get more ideas about what it's like to work in those fields.

Now go back and fill out your "Occupational Information" pages.

In this chapter, you may have gathered information about three to five jobs you'd like to explore. Now you're ready to go out and get some firsthand information by talking to people who actually hold these jobs. This process is called information interviewing, and you'll learn how to do this in the next chapter.

OTHER SOURCES OF INFORMATION

If you're really feeling stuck, you may want to get some extra help by talking to a counselor. A counselor may give you tests to help you discover your skills, interests, and career possibilities and may offer assistance with career planning. Here are some places you can go to find a counselor.

- *Your school guidance office or career center.*
- *A community college career and*

placement center. Any local resident including middle and high school students can usually get free help here. A small fee may be charged for testing.

■ *Private career counselors.* These counselors charge fees for this personalized service. It's best to ask how much the fee is before signing up.

■ *Nonprofit career centers.* Many Y's, scouting organizations, and women's centers offer inexpensive career and job counseling. Look under "Career counseling" in the Yellow Pages. This is *not* the same as an employment agency, which may charge a hefty fee to place you in a job.

4
INTERVIEWING FOR INFORMATION

When you were growing up, your parents probably told you, "Never talk to strangers." That's good advice, but here's one exception to that rule. Talking to people who work in different career fields is a great way to get information about the world of work. Almost everyone, you'll find, likes to talk about his or her job. By asking people how they got where they are (that is, how they made their career choices and how they got their experience) and by observing people at work, you can find out about educational needs, job requirements, salaries, and working conditions. Career experts like Richard Bolles call this process of talking to people about their careers "information interviewing."

Let's say you're interested in becoming a carpenter. Put on a pair of jeans at lunchtime and trek out to the nearest construction site. (*Caution:* Hard-hat areas are off limits to visitors without appointments.) Begin talking to workers during one of their breaks. Ask them what training you will need to be a carpenter and find out what a carpenter does. You'll learn plenty about building houses.

Or perhaps you've been dreaming of a career in the fashion world. You might start your research by talking to a buyer at a small store or boutique. Call ahead to set up an interview. Explain that you're researching different career fields and you're interested in learning about becoming a buyer. Ask if you can make an appointment to talk to the person who buys merchandise for the store. Then put on your good clothes, get there on time, and begin asking questions. Find out what buyers do. Ask how much education or training buyers need. Should you take art courses? Then go on to talk to students and teachers at a college for fashion design. You'll come away with a blueprint for your future in fashion. Or you might decide you don't like the "rag trade" at all. That's okay—better to find out now before you've invested a lot of time and money.

WHY SHOULD YOU CONDUCT AN INFORMATION INTERVIEW?

- *To find out about jobs that are out there.* Naturally, you wouldn't want to investigate all 20,000 kinds of jobs listed in the D.O.T. However, finding out about the ones you're interested in may lead you to jobs you've never thought about.

- *To learn more about other jobs you may want to do.* Let's say you want to learn more about careers in health. Where do you start? Well, you might start with a hospital. Automatically, jobs like nurse, doctor, administrator, and lab technician will come to mind. Have you thought, however, about public relations specialist, clerical assistant, medical coder, maintenance crew member, technician, claims adjuster, credit manager, gift shop operator, volunteer worker, and admissions officer—all jobs necessary to running an efficient and well-organized facility? Maybe you should visit a hospital and talk to some of these workers.

- *To find out what's involved in a job—skills, education, experience, qualifications.* If you want to be a commercial artist, how much school do you need? Can you get by without a college degree in art? Is it better to have practical experience? How about a portfolio? After finding out the answers to these questions, you may discover that a two-year associate degree is just right for you, or that a bit of work experience first would be more helpful.

- *To find out about salaries.* How much can you earn starting out as an electrical engineer? How many years will it take to double your salary? How long does it take to move up? If one of your priorities is making piles of money, then you'll want to work for a private computer company rather than for the federal government where the pay might be considerably less in the long run.

■ *To find out what you might like and dislike about a job.* Say you've always wanted to be a farmer—but you like watching the late, late show every night on television. An interview with a local farmer might convince you that farming means "early-to-bed, early-to-rise." If you're willing to change your late-night routine, then farming could still be for you. However, if rolling out of bed before dawn is out of the question, it's time to look at other careers.

■ *To see if a specific career fits in with your goals, your values, and your vision of a future life-style.* If you want to retire a millionaire by age forty, then don't plan on becoming an elementary school teacher. But if money is not one of your top priorities and you like little kids and enjoy working with finger paints, then you may want to consider teaching kindergarten. If you like working with small groups of children you might look for a job at a private school instead of a big city school system where classes are larger.

■ *To find out where to get more education—colleges, trade schools, apprenticeship programs, community or junior colleges, graduate schools, additional courses.* You can also use information interviewing to decide which school you want to attend. People you've interviewed may have some suggestions about good schools or you can thumb through catalogs in your school guidance office to find appropriate schools. Then visit your top choices and conduct information interviews with students, teachers, and alumni. Asking about grading, school activities, and other facets of campus life will give you a clearer picture of the school than you'd get from reading a catalog or brochure.

■ *To help you decide if you want to start your own business or work for someone else.* When Philip Knight was a student at Stanford University, he had to do a class project for a business course. He developed a business plan for the development and marketing of a lighter, more comfortable, and more durable athletic shoe. Taking his course plan one step further, he went back and talked to his former track coach at the University of Oregon and to other athletes. He discovered there was a need for this type of shoe. Armed with his business plan and the information he collected from his information interviews, Knight, along with his former coach, William Bowerman, started a shoe manufacturing company called Blue Ribbon Shoes that later evolved into Nike. In 1980 Nike sales grossed $269 million. And the comfortable running shoe that you're probably wearing right now may have contributed to this entrepreneur's wealth and independent life-style.

■ *To learn about the world of work—schedules, dress, vocabulary of the trade, and attitudes.* For example, if you hope to sell insurance, a professional agent will tell you that you'll need to wear a suit and you'll have to work evenings and weekends seeing clients. A trade-off is that you may have time off during the day to pursue activities you enjoy—racquetball, swimming, family time, museum visits. You'll also want to pick up some useful trade terms like "annuity," "beneficiary," "premium," "policy," and "term" so you can understand what people in the field are talking about.

■ *To meet people who might later help you get hired.* An interview now may lead to an internship, volunteer position, or paid summer job. Or the person you talk to may even become your mentor—someone who boosts your career by giving you advice and bolstering your confidence. When Thomas Jefferson was starting his government career, Ben Franklin was his guide through the intricate politics of foreign diplomacy. So effective a mentor was Franklin that when he left his post as ambassador to France, Jefferson took his place. If you've ever tuned in to the television show "Fame," you saw the mentor-student relationship between Mr. Shorofsky and a talented young musician. Mr. Shorofsky not only instructed his student in the finer points of playing the piano but also offered career advice and encouragement.

- *To get practice for job interviews.* You'll know your way around an interview—how to dress, act, talk to a stranger about yourself. Information interviewing is, in a way, a rehearsal for a job interview. Practicing now eliminates a lot of the pressure later on.

WHERE TO GO AND WHOM TO TALK TO

Where do you begin your information interviews? Look at how Donald began his search. Donald chose broadcasting as one of his occupational interests. Where did he go to ask questions? Donald thought of local radio stations, a college radio station, and a local cable TV station. After looking up the addresses and telephone numbers of the stations in the phone book, he turned to a new page in his notebook and set it up like this:

PLACES FOR EXPLORATION

Broadcasting

KINDS OF PLACES	NAMES OF PLACES
1. Radio stations	WJOK, Gaithersburg, MD WLMD, Columbia and Laurel, MD WBAL, Baltimore, MD
2. College radio stations	Howard Community College, Columbia, MD American University, Washington, D.C. University of Maryland, College Park, MD National College, Washington, D.C.
3. Cable companies	Howard County Cable, Ellicott City, MD

1. Pick an occupational field that you want to explore, perhaps one that you've already looked up in the D.O.T.
2. Turn to a new page in your career journal and set up a page like Donald's. On the top of your paper write "Places for Exploration." Beneath it put the occupational field you want to explore.
3. In the left-hand column, under "Kinds of Places" list the kinds of places you could visit to find workers to talk to about your occupational choice.

4. In the right-hand column, under "Names of Places" write down actual names and addresses of businesses, schools, and other places in your town or nearby that fit this category.
5. If you get stuck for names of places, try asking people you know for suggestions. Stop by the library and ask the reference librarian for names, addresses, and telephone numbers. Another place you could try is the local chamber of commerce. Or look in the Yellow Pages of the phone book. Donald, for example, could open the Yellow Pages under "Radio stations" to get names and addresses.

Making Contact

The next step is to find people to interview. Donald wrote "Contact List" on a new page of his notebook. Then he made two columns, "Kinds of Workers to Talk to" and "Specific Names." Under "Kinds of Workers to Talk to," he wrote the kinds of workers or job titles of people he wanted to interview (students, a professor of broadcasting, dean of communications). Then Donald called the communications office at National College and asked the secretary for the names of some communications professors and of students who run the radio station. Donald made certain he got the spelling and pronunciation of each person's name, the person's correct title and telephone number. He wrote this information down in his "Specific Names" column. His page looked like this:

CONTACT LIST

Kinds of Persons to Talk to	Specific Names
Students who run the radio station	Bob White Jill Jones
A professor of broadcasting	Professor Wratherbee
The dean of communications	Dean Cromwell
A student studying broadcasting	Sandy Smith
A student disc jockey	Gus Garroway

Now you need to decide which people to interview. First try to identify as many different jobs as you can. Don't consider only the obvious. For example, Donald thought of disc jockeys, station managers, news broadcasters, talk show hosts, and copywriters.

Next you need to identify specific individuals (their names and titles) who do this kind of work or know about these kinds of jobs. To get specific names, you may want to ask friends, teachers, guidance counselors, neighbors, or relatives if they know anyone who works in the field you're exploring. If not, call the place you're going to visit and ask for some names of people to interview. Another good source of names is your local newspaper. For example, Alice is interested in a career writing children's books, so she kept an eye out for articles mentioning local children's book authors. When she saw one, she noted the names of the people mentioned. Then she looked up their telephone numbers in the phone book and called them.

Your community or school bulletin board or newsletter is another place to check. Are there any programs coming up that feature someone you might want to interview? If possible, go hear that person speak and talk to him or her afterward. If you can't attend that particular program, find out how to contact the speaker by calling the organization that sponsored the talk. What other sources of names can you come up with? How about crafts fairs (if you're interested in those occupations), conventions, conferences, brochures, service organizations like the Rotary, the chamber of commerce, the library? You can also write or call trade associations like the American Gem Society or the National Association of Barber Schools (a librarian can help you find addresses) for names of people to talk to and for career information, as well.

GETTING THE INFORMATION

Observing

You may want to start out by just observing a work setting. The next time you need a haircut check out all the different tasks the stylist performs. In addition to cutting hair, he or she may have to know how to work the cash register, give a manicure, or do a chemical hair analysis. At this point, you may even want to ask a few questions and do an on-the-spot information interview. You may try this informal interview in almost any occupational field. Go to a park and watch a park ranger lead a tour group, visit an eye doctor and watch as he or she examines your eyes, or observe a travel agent helping a customer decide on a vacation spot. Then ask questions: How do you become a park ranger (eye doctor, travel agent)? What kind of advancement opportunities are available? What do you like or dislike about your work?

For some career fields, however, this kind of informal observation may not be possible. For instance, you can't drop in on an oceanographer who's making a deep sea dive, walk into an engineering company that handles U.S. defense contracts, or stop by a lawyer's office to observe the activity there. For those interviews, you'll have to make an appointment.

INFORMATION INTERVIEWING

Making Appointments

Try to get the name of a worker you can interview. If you can't find a name, ask the secretary for one when you call for an appointment.

Brenda, for example, wanted to talk to an airline flight attendant. She called the Delta Airlines public relations office and spoke to the director of public relations.

BRENDA: Hello, my name is Brenda Jones, and I go to Wilson High School. I'm interested in learning more about becoming a flight attendant. Would it be possible for me to talk to one or two of your flight attendants?

DIRECTOR: If you'll give me your name, address, and telephone number, I'll send you some information about working for an airline and have one of our flight attendants call you.

Brenda gave the director her name, address, and phone number and thanked her for her help. When the flight attendant called back, Brenda set up an appointment to talk to her during one of the flight attendant's stops in Brenda's city. If the flight attendant hadn't returned Brenda's call, Brenda planned to check back with the director within two weeks after her initial phone call.

Getting Your Questions Ready

Once you've set up an appointment, you need to decide what you're going to ask during the interview. Always write down a list of questions to bring with you. Remember, in an information interview, you're the one asking questions: you're the interviewer, a Barbara Walters or Mike Wallace, trying to gather as much information as you can. People like to talk about themselves and their jobs, so don't worry, there will be plenty to discuss. Here are a few questions you may want to ask:

Questions for Information Interviews

1. How did you get into this field?
2. What type of preparation did you need? How much school? Any special training?
3. What different tasks do you perform during an average day?
4. What do you like best about your job?
5. What do you like least about your job?
6. Do you need any special tools, equipment, or clothing?
7. What kind of working conditions do you have here? Hours? Amount of stress?
8. What is the salary range for a person starting in this field? (*Don't* ask the person how much he or she makes!)
9. What is the future outlook for jobs in this field?
10. What other kinds of jobs are there in this field? What are they like?
11. What other companies do the same kind of work? Do you know anyone there whom I could talk to?
12. Can you suggest other people in the field to speak with? (Try to get at least two names.) How can I contact them?

Now start a page titled "More Questions for Information Interviewing" and write down any specific questions relating to your career field.

Making a Practice Run

Before the interview, you may want to do a test run with a friend or a family member. Try out these questions on your mother and father to find out about their jobs; or interview an older relative or friend. If you can't find anyone to practice on, try talking into a tape recorder. Play it back and listen to yourself. Visualize the interview as you listen. If there are rough spots, smooth them out and try again.

Deciding What to Wear

If you plan to go into a law firm, and you're a guy, you probably will want to wear a suit or a nice sweater and slacks. If you're a girl, you probably will want to wear a suit, dress, or a sharp-looking skirt and blouse. On the other hand, when you're interviewing auto mechanics, jeans are perfectly acceptable; just make sure they're not the grungy, grass-stained ones you wear to play soccer. Try to picture what the person you're going to interview will be wearing and then dress more or less the same way.

Being Prepared

Bring a pencil and pad to jot down notes. Later on, you will be able to go back and check out information, and the person you interview will be pleased to think that what he or she says is important enough to write down.

GOING ON THE INFORMATION INTERVIEW

- *Be on time.* Common courtesy demands that you arrive promptly for your meeting. A potential employer might reasonably think that if you're late for a meeting, you'll be late for a job. You certainly wouldn't want to make the wrong impression.
- *First impressions count—even with the secretary.* Offer a friendly hello and tell him or her that you have a meeting with Mr. or Ms. Blank.
- *If you have to wait, pick up a magazine and glance through it.* If there are any company pamphlets or brochures in the reception room, you may want to take a look through these, too. You may come up with more questions for your interview and additional helpful information.

The Interview

- *Stand up and shake hands when you meet the person you're interviewing.* Remember to have a firm handshake—no bone-crushers or limp wrists, please. Smile, look him or her in the eye and introduce yourself. (For example, Donald said, "Hi. I'm Donald Tyson. Dean

Cromwell suggested I speak with you.")
It's a good idea to mention how you got
your interviewee's name, just as Donald
did.

■ *Try some icebreakers.* Everyone is
nervous when meeting a new person. It's
hard to think of what to say to a stranger.
Chances are your interviewee will feel the
same way. Using icebreakers is really
making small talk. Try chatting briefly
about the good directions you had for
getting there, the pictures on the walls, or
even the old standby—the weather.

■ *Take out your pad and pencil and begin
asking the questions you've brought.* Ask
one question at a time and be sure to
allow the person enough time to answer
them. You may want to take notes. Don't
be afraid to ask any questions that pop
into your head, too.

■ *Make eye contact.* Look at the person
you're talking to. Don't let your eyes
wander all around the room. But don't
stare your interviewee down. Good eye
contact makes an individual feel important
and shows that you're interested in what
he or she has to say.

■ *Be considerate of your interviewee's time.*
The person you're talking to may have a
busy schedule, so keep within the time
allotted. If it looks as though you're taking
up more time than planned, make sure it's
okay. Asking "Do you have time for a few
more questions?" would be a good way of
doing this.

Ending the Interview

- *Signal the end of the interview.* When you're done asking questions, ask for the names of other people you might talk to for further information.
- *Say thank you.* When it's time to leave, shake hands again and thank the person for his or her time and information.

Following Up

- *Send a handwritten thank-you note.* Use plain stationery. Save your purple letter paper with dancing pink elephants for notes to your friends. Once again thank the person you interviewed. Also, you might mention that you learned a lot that will help you make a career choice.

Donald sent this note to Dean Cromwell after his information interview:

March 20, 19___

Dean Cromwell
Communications Department
National College
Washington, DC 20416

Dear Dean Cromwell:

Thank you for taking the time to talk to me last Tuesday. The information you gave me was very helpful. I plan to meet with the people you suggested later this month. I enjoyed talking to you and visiting the college.

Sincerely,

Donald Tyson

Keeping Records

Start an Information Interview Diary in your notebook and take a few minutes after each interview to fill it out. Write down the date of the interview and the interviewee's name, address, and telephone number. (When you're looking for a job or internship, you may want to call on these people again.) Then note the date you sent a thank-you note. Make a few notes on what you learned from each interview, and if you want more information about a career, jot down what you need and whom you can talk with to get it. Use a new notebook page for each interview.

Note how Donald set up his Information Interview Diary. Set yours up in the same way, using two pages, if necessary.

INFORMATION INTERVIEW DIARY

—BROADCASTING—

DATE	INTERVIEWEE	DISCOVERIES
2/22	Dean Cromwell National College Congressional Ave. NW, Wash., DC 20416 202-555-2000	1. This is a 4-year course Need to take Eng. courses, speech, journalism. 2. Very popular & growing field. Should be a lot of jobs opening up but competition will be stiff. 3. Cable will bring more jobs. Number of cable companies expanding.

After all your interviews are finished, you'll have a pretty good idea of the type of job that appeals to you and what you'll need to do to get that kind of job. Or maybe you'll have decided that working for someone else is not for you and you want to explore owning your own business. If so, take a look at Chapter Five: Beginning Your Own Business. Chapter Six: Writing Resumes and Filling Out Applications will give suggestions on filling out applications or submitting resumes for jobs where you'll be working for others.

OTHER INFO I NEED	HOW TO GET INFO	THANK YOU
What it's like to actually work at a station.	1. Call up local radio show or station & see if I can talk to newscaster. 2. Call up college station & talk to students.	2/24

5
BEGINNING YOUR OWN BUSINESS

Most of us go through high school thinking there are only two options after graduation: continuing on to college, trade school, or some other type of education, or going to work for someone else.

Have you ever thought of still another option—being an entrepreneur, owning, operating, and managing a business for profit? Being your own boss isn't such a farfetched idea.

Timothy Putman started his own business when he was fourteen. "I had worked a lot of jobs—being a cashier, working on a farm, and doing carpentry—but none of them were satisfying. I think I got the idea of being my own boss when I was weeding strawberries one summer for twenty-five cents a row. I thought: If this is what it's like to work for someone else, I never want to do it again." He knew he wanted to make money on his own, and he started out by repairing old bikes and selling them. Soon he had $100 in a bank account and he was on his way to becoming a successful entrepreneur.

Meanwhile, in high school, Tim took graphic arts courses and soon developed a plan for a silk-screening and printing business. "I realized that it was a big industry and that there could be a lot of money in it. Yet the basic supplies to start out only cost around a hundred fifty dollars." He showed his plans to his teachers, some businesspeople he knew, and friends. After collecting comments and more information, he developed a strategy to begin operations. Then he opened T. P. Screen Printing and began making bumper stickers, T-shirts, and other silk-screened items in his home. He soon hired two friends to handle sales and planned to begin a mail-order service.

"You have to feel comfortable making decisions and realize that even the bad ones will allow you to learn from them," Tim points out. "You have to realize that you can't do things by yourself. You need other people's help." Although Tim doesn't expect to become a millionaire overnight, he enjoys the challenge of making money and putting out a quality product as an entrepreneur.

Maybe you don't plan on going into business while you're in school as Tim did. Perhaps you want to start your business after graduation or after college. You may even be considering a profession like lawyer, accountant, engineer, writer, or doctor. Often, these people work for themselves, too. In any of these careers it's helpful to know a bit about starting a business.

Entrepreneurs make up a large chunk of the business community, representing 95 percent of all businesses in the United States. (The other 5 percent is made up of big businesses like General Motors and IBM.) Approximately 1,200 new businesses are formed each day.

DO YOU HAVE WHAT IT TAKES TO BE AN ENTREPRENEUR?

Are you the entrepreneurial type? To be an entrepreneur you must:

- *Be willing to take educated risks.* You must be prepared to risk your time, money, and ego to try to make a business work. Being an educated risk taker means more than going with the roll of the dice, leaving things to chance. You must make plans and have good skills like Timothy Putman.
- *Be willing to work hard.* Be prepared to put in long hours to get your business started. You might have to round up customers, keep records, sweep floors, deliver orders, and manage the money. All of this takes more time and work than you'd put in if you were working for someone else.
- *Be independent and self-motivated.* You must be able to make decisions on your own. Remember you're your own boss. No one's going to make you get up in the morning and start working. You've got to want to do that yourself.

- *Be self-confident.* You have to believe in yourself and believe that you will be successful even when business is bad—even to the point where you'll have to put in your own money to show a bank or a customer that you're committed.
- *Be willing to ask for help when you need it.* You can't possibly know everything yourself, so you must know when and how to get help. You may need to get a bank loan or find out how to balance your books or hire someone to help with a job you can't do.
- *Be focused*—or a goal setter. Successful entrepreneurs pursue one goal at a time. For example, it's not wise to go into business selling hot dogs and hats at the same time. You've got to concentrate on either the food business (hot dogs) or the selling of hats. Don't move on to another goal until you've completed the first.
- *Be creative.* You must be ready to think up new ways to do things and new approaches to problems. You may have to make your product or service better and/or cheaper than that of your competitors.
- *Have technical knowledge.* Tim Putman had to take courses in graphic arts before he could open his silk-screening shop. You've got to know about the product or service you're going to offer. If you're going to design software for computers, for example, you've got to know how computers work.
- *Have business knowledge.* You have to know how to operate a business: pay bills,

set prices for products and services,
develop a rapport with customers, keep
books, market and advertise your
business, and handle all the other details
of running a small company. According to
the Small Business Administration, most
new businesses fail because the owners
don't know enough about how to run a
business.

To see how you rate as a potential entrepreneur,
answer the following questions. First take out your
career journal and title a page "Entrepreneurial
Checklist." Number down the left side of the page
from 1 to 23. Then make four columns across your
page, like this.

ENTREPRENEURIAL CHECKLIST

	Very True	Fairly True	Rather False	Absolutely False
1.				
2.				
3. . .				

Here are some questions about the kind of person
you consider yourself to be. Check the column that
tells how true or false each statement is for you.

1. I want to be rewarded for my successes,
   but I don't mind taking the blame if
   things go wrong.

2. I like to know the results of tests as quickly as possible.
3. I am pretty sure of who I am, what I can do, and what I want to do with my life.
4. I try to learn all I can about selling products or services.
5. I am good at solving real-life problems.
6. I'm an "idea" person; I keep thinking up new things to do or new ways to do things.
7. I am in control of my life; I don't just let life do things to me.
8. I need to keep succeeding but only by my own efforts.
9. I like a standard to measure myself by so that I can know how well I'm doing.
10. I am good at setting goals and figuring out how to achieve them.
11. I am responsible for my actions and the consequences of those actions.
12. I like a challenge that is hard but that I can probably meet if I stretch myself a bit.
13. I plan and organize my life.
14. I pretty much go along with what people tell me I should do with my life.
15. If I could win a prize, either by rolling dice with a one-in-three chance of winning or by working out the solution to a problem with the same chance of winning, I would choose to roll the dice rather than work on the problem.
16. I don't like challenging activities.
17. I am not good at organizing things.
18. I like to try to do things that are so

difficult that I need a lot of luck to succeed.

19. I accept other people's advice on most things, even if they're not experts.
20. Once I finish my education, I just want to make as much money as possible.
21. I really admire people who are prepared to risk all their money in a crap game.

(Adapted from "Introducing Entrepreneurship as a Career Option into a High School Curriculum," prepared by American Management Associations for the U.S. Small Business Administration, Office of Advocacy.)

If you answered "fairly true" or "very true" to most of questions 1 through 13, and "rather false" or "absolutely false" to most of questions 14 through 21, you have the makings of an entrepreneur.

If you're still thinking about becoming an entrepreneur, you may want to look at the chart below to see some of the advantages and disadvantages of owning your own business.

ADVANTAGES OF OWNING YOUR OWN BUSINESS

1. Being your own boss and not having to answer to anyone else.
2. Having a flexible work schedule.
3. Reaping a larger share of the profits. In other words, if the business makes money, you get more of it.
4. Avoiding a bureaucracy. You don't have to go through ten people to make a decision.

5. Satisfying your special interests. Just as Tim uses his graphic arts skills, you could put your own skills and interests to work.
6. Creating a new product, testing a new idea, starting a new service.
7. Providing a quality service or product that meets your standards.
8. Increasing professional and personal contacts by developing a network of customers, merchants, and other professional services.

DISADVANTAGES OF OWNING YOUR OWN BUSINESS

1. Having a lot of demands on your time. You might end up working twenty hours a day and not taking a vacation.
2. Dealing with employee problems.
3. Increasing your liabilities. Your machinery can break, someone could have an accident at your place, and so forth.
4. Raising capital. You'll have to come up with money to finance your operations.
5. Risking losses. Sometimes you lose money before you earn it, or you just don't make any money.
6. Coping with frustration. The more responsibility you handle, the more frustrations you're likely to encounter as clients don't show up, orders aren't delivered on time, and so on.
7. Adding strain to the family by not having time for them because your business

requires so much work. Using family funds to keep the company going can cause tension, too.

8. Handling excessive paperwork. Government regulations and good business practices may require filling out tons of forms and keeping a lot of records.

9. Risking personal failure. Even if you've worked very hard and done everything possible, the business still may not succeed.

If you're really serious about pursuing your own business, the best way to get information and help is to go out and talk to entrepreneurs. This is another form of information interviewing. (For a complete review of the information interview, go back over Chapter Four.) Here are some tips to keep in mind.

TIPS FOR INTERVIEWING ENTREPRENEURS

1. Identify the kind of business you're interested in.

2. Now identify some local businesses that are doing what you want to do. Look in the Yellow Pages or contact people you know.

3. Get the name of an entrepreneur to talk to by phoning the business or talking to someone you know.

4. Call or write to make an appointment.

5. Explain that you are doing career

research for a project on owning your own
business.
6. Think of questions to ask ahead of time.
   Write them down.
7. Get to the appointment on time.
8. Remember to write a thank-you note
   afterward.

Save a few pages in your journal on which to jot
down some notes about each interview—whom you
spoke to and what you learned—just as you did for
your information interviews in Chapter Four.

Here are some questions Lynn prepared to ask the
owner of dog kennel. You might want to use these
questions, too.

Questions for Interviewing a Business Owner

1. How did you get into this business?
2. How long have you been in business?
3. What preparation did you need? Did you
   need any special training? What kind of
   courses did you take?
4. What did you do before owning your
   own business?
5. When did you first decide to be an
   entrepreneur?
6. What tasks do you perform in an
   average workday?
7. What do you like best about being in
   business?
8. What do you like least about being in
   business?
9. What hours do you work?

10. Is there a lot of stress in your work?
11. Can you make money in this kind of business?
12. What does it take to get started?
13. Who are some other people in this business that I can talk to?

Lynn wrote down the answers to these questions in her career journal on a page titled "Information Interview—Posh Pooch Kennels."

This journal can be the start of your own business plan. Use it to jot down any ideas you have about what kind of business you would like to start and how you might go about it. The U.S. Small Business Administration has several free booklets on how to write a business plan; you'll find the address at the end of this chapter.

Developing a Business Plan

Here's a brief outline of what a business plan looks like. If you have an idea for a business you want to start, use this outline to develop your thoughts. Copy this outline down in your notebook and try to answer as many questions as you can.

BUSINESS PLAN

Name of business   Address
Name of owner   Telephone number

Purpose statement. A specific description of the business, product, service, or idea. (Example: a boarding service for pets.)

The company's goals. What is your business supposed to accomplish? (Example: to provide boarding and grooming services for dogs and cats and to sell toys, food, leashes, and other products for pets.)

The market. Who are your customers?

The competition. What other products or services on the market are like yours?

Location. Where will your business be located?

Management. Who will run the business? What are the specific qualifications for this job?

Employees. Who will work for you? What types of jobs will there be? How many employees will you need?

How will you sell (market) your product or service? Will you sell through your own salespeople or through agents?

How much will you charge for your product or service?

Break-even analysis. How much will you need to sell to make a profit?

Time line. When do you plan to accomplish the following tasks?

Task   Date
1. Obtain your license.
2. Buy your supplies.
3. Hire employees.
4. Open your doors for business.
5. Deliver the first product or service.

Financing. Where will your investment money come from?

1. What is your monthly budget for the first twelve months of operation? (Start-up costs will include licensing, supplies, space, phone, and so forth.)
2. How much money do you hope to make? Will this be sufficient for what you want to do? (That is, will you be able to make a living from your company?)

These are the kinds of questions you'll have to answer as you develop your business plan. If you're in the "just thinking" stage of opening a business, you won't have to answer all of these questions now. But if you're planning to open a business soon, you'll need to have most of the answers. You don't have to do this all alone, however. You can get help from SCORE (Senior Corps of Retired Executives), a volunteer service of the U.S. Small Business Administration (SBA). There are branches of both SCORE and SBA all over the country (see Other Special Resources at the end of this chapter). You can also attend free or inexpensive SBA workshops at nearby colleges.

Then, when you're really serious, you may want to visit an accountant or a lawyer or both. An accountant will help you predict future growth of your business. A lawyer will advise you on what type of business you should set up:

■ *Sole proprietorship:* One owner is solely

responsible for debts and receives all profits.

- *Partnership:* Two or more owners share the debts, profits, and losses.
- *Corporation:* An enterprise formed by shareholders and chartered to exist separately from its owners so that the corporation is liable for debts. Profits may be distributed to shareholders when available.

Something to consider for the future, when you're experienced and have money to invest, is buying an existing business or even a franchise of a big business like McDonald's, Hertz-Rent-A-Car, or Holiday Inns.

GETTING MONEY TO START YOUR BUSINESS

Jackie Pikowski had been an avid collector of baseball and football cards and movie memorabilia since she was two years old. At age fourteen, she decided to start a card and movie memorabilia business. She talked over her idea with her older sister who owned a management consulting firm. Her sister agreed to lend Jackie the money to start her new venture if she operated her new enterprise like a business. Jackie called her new company, which she operated out of her home, My Sister's Card Shop. At age seventeen, Jackie was ready to enter college and continue the business on a part-time basis. She had multiplied her original $4,000 investment into an inventory worth more than $40,000 retail. Jackie has been featured in magazine articles and has appeared on television to talk about her success.

When Jackie Pikowski wanted to start her business she used an obvious funding resource, her sister. She had a good idea about what she wanted to do. Before you approach anyone for funding, you should have a solid financial plan. What are some sources you could tap to get some start-up cash?

Sources Of Start-up Cash

- *Your family.* Can any family members or friends of the family help you get started?
- *Your personal savings account.* Timothy Putman used his own money to start his silk-screening business.
- *Informal investors.* Maybe there are people in your community, church, or synagogue who have made money as entrepreneurs and might be interested in investing in your company. Approach these people with your plan and see if they'd be willing to give you a loan or perhaps make an investment.
- *Commercial banks and savings and loan companies.* To borrow money from a bank, you would have to have a well-thought-out business plan and some money of your own. Since there are age minimums and credit and residency requirements to get this type of loan, it's best to have your plan looked over by a knowledgeable business person or an SBA or SCORE adviser before you head to your bank.

- *Suppliers or vendors.* These are people who will give you merchandise or supplies on credit. To get information about suppliers, check with local business associations and other businesses in the same field.
- *Small Business Administration.* If you're turned down by banks, the SBA has guaranteed loans and sometimes direct financing. Loans to women and minority business owners are available and particularly encouraged.
- *Partners.* Look for a partner to go into a business with you. You will share costs as well as profits (and triumphs as well as headaches).

In your career journal list the names of three people whom you can talk to about funding. Write down a brief note about what you will say to them.

Other Special Resources

U.S. SMALL BUSINESS ADMINISTRATION, 1441 "L" Street NW, Washington, DC 20416 (202-653-6365). Look in the Yellow Pages of your phone directory for the office nearest you; then call or write your local office or the Washington office for such free publications as the following:

"Checklist for Going into Business"
"Sound Cash Management and Borrowing"
"Business Plan for Small Service Firms"
"Business Plan for Small Manufacturers"

"Business Plan for Small Construction Firms"
"Selecting the Legal Structure for Your Firm"
"Marketing Checklist for Small Retailers"
"Incorporating a Small Business"

SBA ANSWER DESK (800-368-5855). A free hot line for any questions you may have about owning, operating, or managing a small business.

OFFICE OF ECONOMIC DEVELOPMENT. Your county or city government may have an Office of Economic Development. Here you can find out who your competitors are and what your service market is (that is, who lives in your area and if they're likely to patronize your business).

CHAMBER OF COMMERCE. The chamber of commerce is a network of business people in the community. You can go to the chamber to talk to other business owners and get information about the local marketplace. Chamber members can also refer you to other resources like lawyers and accountants

BUSINESS DEVELOPMENT CENTERS AT LOCAL COLLEGES AND UNIVERSITIES. These centers provide information about owning and operating small businesses.

THE LIBRARY. Your public library has books on starting your own business.

AWED. American Women's Economic Development Corporation, 60 East 42nd Street, New York, NY 10165 (212-692-9100). AWED is a nonprofit organization that provides counseling to women who want to start their own businesses. AWED helps prospective businesswomen with marketing tools and gives legal and financial advice.

The most important thing you can do if you want to become an entrepreneur is to make owning a business your goal. Set a target date, even if it's several years away, for when you want to begin your business. Think about what further education and skills, if any, you'll need to meet that goal. Will you need any special kind of work experience? How much money will you have to save to start your own business? How will you earn that money?

Being an entrepreneur is not for everyone. It's a difficult road to take, but a very rewarding one for those who have personal drive and like taking calculated risks.

6 WRITING RESUMES AND FILLING OUT APPLICATIONS

You wouldn't think of traveling to Europe without a passport. Nor would you think of going out into the business world without a resume. Just as a passport identifies you personally, a resume shows who you are professionally. It also tells people what you can do. It may not contain your picture or your fingerprints, but it will describe the experience and skills unique to you.

A resume is a one- or two-page summary of your work experiences, education, skills, and accomplishments. It's really an advertisement for yourself—a document that says, "Hire me. Here's what

I've done, what I can do, and what I would like to do." It's something like a preview of a movie. If you see clips from a motion picture and like what you see, you'll go to the movie when it comes to your neighborhood theater. Well, it's the same with a resume. If an employer likes the brief glimpse he gets of you by reading your resume, he'll probably ask you in for an interview so he can meet you and learn more about you.

WHY WRITE A RESUME?

- *Just getting your accomplishments down on paper is a confidence booster.* Most people are surprised at all they've done.

- *A resume is a marketing tool.* It's a way for you to advertise your strengths to an employer. With a resume you can toot your own horn without sounding like Bozo the Braggart.

- *If you're starting your own business, a resume can help you get a loan at a bank.* Your resume shows the loan officer that you have a track record, that you have already accomplished something, and that you're likely to continue to work hard in the future.

- *A resume can serve as a reminder during a job interview.* Suppose you're feeling a bit nervous during an interview and your mind goes blank—you can't remember the skills you used on your job as a library page. All you have to do is look down at your resume and see exactly what you did—shelve books; check books in and out.

- *You can also use a resume as a memory jogger when you fill out applications.* A quick glance at your resume will give you the answers to questions about where you worked, what you did, for whom, and when. You won't have to scratch your head thinking of words to write; you can copy them from your resume.

- *A resume can work as a calling card.* After you've left the interview, the employer has a reminder of what you can do, as well as your name, address, and telephone number.

Take a look at the Personal Inventory chart on the next page. On a new page of your notebook, write "My Personal Inventory" on the top line. Then on the left side of your journal page copy down the categories (job objective, education, relevant course-work, experience, and so forth), taking care to leave several blank lines between the different categories. (Use a couple of notebook pages, if necessary.) After doing that, write the answers to the questions next to each category. Later, you will use these sheets to prepare your resume or to help you fill out applications.

PERSONAL INVENTORY

HEADING	NAME Address Telephone
JOB OBJECTIVE	What kind of job are you looking for? (Look at your Career Journal at the end of Chapter Four.)
EDUCATION	What schools have you completed or are about to complete? (List high school, technical schools, special coursework outside of school.) Include name of the school(s), city, state, and completion date, kind of diploma or degree granted.
RELEVANT COURSEWORK	What special courses did you take that relate to the kind of job you want?
EXPERIENCE	List your three main skill areas. (Take this from the skills area of your notebook.) You may be able to think of only two skill areas—that's fine, too.

Skill Area I: _____
   (Where did you use this skill?
   List any jobs, volunteer
   positions, school projects, etc.,
   where you used this skill.)

Skill Area II: _____
(Where did you use this skill?
List any jobs, volunteer
positions, school projects, etc.,
where you used this skill.)

Skill Area III: _____
(Where did you use this skill?
List any jobs, volunteer
positions, school projects, etc.
where you used this skill.)

INTERESTS — List your hobbies, activities, and special interests.

AFFILIATIONS/ MEMBERSHIPS — Do you belong to any clubs, organizations, or community groups?

AWARDS — List awards and honors like National Honor Society and civic awards.

REFERENCES — List teachers, employers, community leaders, club officers, clergy, or anyone who would be willing to write a good letter of recommendation for you. Check this out with them first to be certain. (You can list three people as references.)

This Personal Inventory sheet will be the basis for your resume. Now let's look at resume formats.

GETTING THERE WITH STYLE

Just as you choose the best kind of luggage—suitcase, duffel bag, suit bag, or backpack—to carry your clothes in on a trip, you will want to choose the best style of resume to suit your experience for finding a job. There are three basic formats for writing a resume—chronological, functional, and combination.

Chronological Resume

"Chronological" means "arranged in order of time." A chronological resume lists your work experience in reverse order of time. That is, your last job comes first, then your next-to-the-last, and so on.

If you have a steady job history, this is an excellent resume format to use because it shows how your work experience has grown. It's not a good type of resume to use if you haven't held a steady job or haven't worked very regularly, because this type of resume stresses the dates and places you worked. It immediately shows all the gaps in your employment record. It is, however, the kind of resume employers are most familiar with and it's the easiest type to write. Now look at the chronological resume on the next page.

TERRI BERGER

5736 Broken Lane
Center City, New Jersey 08502
(201) 555-2525 home
(201) 555-1212 work

CAREER OBJECTIVE	Sales / Training Program
EDUCATION	Center City High School, Center City, New Jersey, June 1985, Honor Society
EXPERIENCE	*Sales Clerk,* Thrifty Foods Store, Center City, N.J. September 1984 to present, summer and part-time while attending school
	Take inventory control. Keep store records. Operate busy cash register. Serve customers.
	Sales Clerk, La Belle Dress Shop, Center City, N.J. 1983–84, summers and after school
	Waited on customers. Assisted with selections. Developed good customer relations. Wrote up sales orders. Assisted in setting up displays.
AFFILIATION	Junior Achievement, Center City High School 1983–85
REFERENCES	Available on request

Advantages of a Chronological Resume

- It's easy to write.
- It's easy to read.
- Employers are familiar with this kind of resume.
- It shows steady progression in your work history.

Functional Resumes

Rather than emphasizing the dates and places you've worked, a functional resume stresses skills such as selling, typing, repairing, speaking, data processing, and writing. On this type of resume you pick out two or three of your strongest skill areas (listed on your Personal Inventory sheet) and place your accomplishments and the jobs you've held under the appropriate skill headings. For example, under the category "selling" you might put your experience selling candy for the school fund-raiser; then under "art" you might tell about the posters you made for the city fair. The skills you choose should be related to your career goal.

The advantage of a functional resume is that you can emphasize the skills that match the job you're pursuing. Also, you may never have held a steady job or jobs; your experience may be scattered over volunteer work, school projects, and hobbies as well as paid jobs. A functional resume makes the most of a spotty work history by picking out what's most important from what you've done and putting it first. If you have enough work experience, you can even leave out jobs that aren't relevant.

Take a look at the functional resume on the following page.

BONNIE SONTAG
6789 Maple Avenue
Sea City, California 95616
(916) 555-1122

JOB OBJECTIVE

Responsible job using my secretarial skills and knowledge of office procedures.

EXPERIENCE

Clerical Skills

As office worker with Timely Temporaries, typed letters, operated adding machine, dictaphone, and photocopier. Maintained filing system, answered phones, distributed mail.

As volunteer office worker in busy hospital, answered phones, typed business correspondence, filed, used duplicating machines, collated and mailed materials.

Bookkeeping Skills

Typed bills for customers in bookkeeping office of manufacturing company for Timely Temporaries.

As treasurer of school club, kept books—records of expenditures and disbursements. Wrote checks. Made deposits for group.

EDUCATION

Ocean High School, Sea City, California 1985

INTERESTS

Jogging, skiing, reading, singing in choir.

REFERENCES

Available on request.

Advantages of a Functional Resume

- It highlights your skills.
- You don't have to worry about a sporadic work record.
- You can leave off jobs that aren't relevant to your job goal.
- You don't have to be concerned with dates or places.

Combination Resume

A combination resume is just what its name implies. It's a mixture of your skills with a chronological list of jobs you've held. It combines the best of both kinds of resumes. It allows you to show what you can do (your skills), and it tells where you've developed these skills (your work history—dates and places). This is an excellent choice for students who have some work experience and want to highlight certain skills. Here's an example of a combination resume.

DONALD TYSON
4653 Flower Avenue
Old Court, Virginia 22010
703-555-1234

OBJECTIVE   Position using my audiovisual and media skills. Am quick to learn, enthusiastic, self-reliant and responsible.

EDUCATION   Senior, Old Court High School, Old Court, VA

SPECIAL SKILLS   Workshops in 35mm. photography, darkroom, and drama at Virginia Center for the Arts.

Can operate video tape recorder, movie and slide projectors (including Super 8 and 16mm.), and most other audiovisual equipment.

EXPERIENCE

Audiovisual Skills   As audiovisual aide for high school, operated and maintained all audiovisual equipment for teachers.

Action-photographed games for slide presentation as photographer for state championship soccer team. Took and developed still shots.

Produced, directed, filmed, and edited Super 8 live action movie. Won first place in county school film festival.

Media Skills

As page at public library, shelve, check in, and check out books. Operate computer system.

Operate computer as media aide in school library. Shelve books, check books in and out. Show students how to use catalogs and microfilm.

WORK HISTORY

Page, Old Court Library, Old Court, VA, 1981 to present, part-time after school.

Photographer, Old Court Soccer Team, 1982.

Audiovisual Aide, Old Court High School, Old Court, VA, 1981.

AWARDS

First Place in County Film Festival.

AFFILIATIONS

Thespian Society
Media Club

REFERENCES

Available on request.

Advantages of a Combination Resume

- It highlights your skills right up front where an employer can see them.
- It gives the employer a list of places where you've worked.
- You can leave out unrelated jobs.

Which Resume Style Is Best for You?

Go over the list of advantages for each of the three types of resumes. Look carefully at the sample resumes. Now decide which format suits you best. If you can't make up your mind, try answering these questions.

1. Do I have a steady work history? Does my experience relate to the job I want now? (If the answer to these questions is yes, write a chronological resume.)
2. Is all my experience scattered among school projects, volunteer jobs, and/or low-paying jobs like baby-sitting and newspaper delivery? (If the answer is yes, write a functional resume.)
3. Have you held some paid jobs relating to your career goal and done some volunteer and/or school or community projects? (If the answer is yes, do a combination resume.)

GET READY, GET SET, WRITE

Now that you've chosen the type of resume that suits your needs, you're ready to start writing. First read the tips below. Then go back and transfer the information from your Personal Inventory to the appropriate place on your resume. Turn to a new page in your notebook and write your own resume, using the model resume as a guide.

Writing Tips

1. Use active verbs to describe what you've done. (For example: prepared speech, designed program, organized club, developed budget, wrote publicity, computed income, planned event.) See the list of active verbs below and look back at the Skills page in your journal.

Active Verbs

planned	initiated	performed
organized	evaluated	played
led	analyzed	staged
painted	created	typed
wrote	designed	filed
edited	composed	prepared
built	informed	ordered
constructed	taught	compiled
assembled	trained	categorized

Active Verbs cont.

calculated	researched	counseled
recorded	developed	listened

operated	negotiated	invented
monitored	persuaded	fashioned
diagnosed	motivated	shaped
installed	sold	improved
programmed		
debugged		

2. Don't use the pronoun "I."
3. Don't use full sentences.
4. Leave out "a" and "the." (For instance, don't write "I planned a party for the choir fund-raiser." Instead, write "Planned party for choir fund-raiser.")
5. Don't include personal data like your age, height, weight, or birth date. This information isn't necessary and may prejudice the employer against you.

APPEARANCES COUNT

Just as the clothes you wear say something about you, so does your resume. If it's all smudgy or looks as if it fell in the mud, you're not going to get that interview. Very often you send your resume out before an employer ever meets you, so remember that first impressions do count. Before typing up your final copy, read over the following list of Do's and Don'ts.

Resume Do's and Don'ts

1. Use 8½-by-11-inch unlined paper. Try to use a good-quality typing paper—not onionskin or erasable bond. It should be a neutral color (white, off-white, light beige, or gray). Stay away from shocking pink unless you want to work for a carnival.

2. Leave plenty of white space. Make sure you have margins of at least one inch all the way around the page.

3. Type your resume. Be sure your typewriter is in good condition and its ribbon is dark. Use plain type, not fancy script. If you can't type, have a friend or relative do it for you. If need be, look in the Yellow Pages to find a typist to do it for you. It may cost you a few dollars but it will pay off in the end.

4. Check for grammatical or spelling errors. Make sure everything is spelled correctly.

5. Keep your resume to one or two pages.

6. Use a good-quality duplication or printing service when making copies of your resume. A dark, spotty copy from the community center photocopy machine may be cheap, but it won't win you any job interviews.

The Critical Eye

It's a good idea to have someone else read over your resume before you start handing it out. You want to make sure that what you've written makes sense, is easy to read, and is grammatically correct. You could give it to someone you know who's in business or to a friend or relative to evaluate. You can also go to the career center at a college, community college, or high school and have a counselor look it over. Check to see what the reader has learned about you from your resume. Does this match the picture you want to present?

Here's a checklist to use for evaluating your resume.

RESUME CHECKLIST

1. Does your resume give a good picture of your skills?
2. Is it neat? Is it good-looking with a lot of white space?
3. Did you use active verbs?
4. Does it stress the positive?
5. Is it factual?
6. Does it really give a good picture of who you are?

Consider your resume from an employer's point of view. Employers use resumes to pick people for a job and to eliminate others from consideration. For each ad in the newspaper, an employer may get two hundred responses. How will he or she decide whom to interview? The employer, after looking over the resumes, will toss out ones that aren't relevant to the job—those resumes that do not present an image of a person he or she wants to hire. The first ones to go are those that are too messy or too difficult to read, so spending the extra effort getting someone else to do a critique of your resume is well worthwhile.

COVER LETTERS

A cover letter is a short letter that you send out with your resume. This letter serves as an introduction and lets the company know what job you're applying for. It also highlights your experience and skills, especially those that are relevant to the job.

Basic Format for a Cover Letter

Your street address
City, State Zip code
Date

Name of person, Title
Company
Street address
City, State Zip code.

Dear Mr. or Ms. . . .:

First paragraph—State the job you're applying for and mention where or from whom you heard about the job.

Second paragraph—Describe your strong points, experience, and skills relevant to the job you're applying for.

Third paragraph—Indicate that you are enclosing your resume. Suggest a meeting. Thank this person for his or her consideration.

Very truly yours,

Your name

Here's a cover letter one student sent with his resume to a local radio station.

2378 Bullwinkle Boulevard
Bethesda, Maryland 20814
March 17, 198—

Rick Wayne, Editor
The Weekly News
7340 Whisper Avenue
Laurel, Maryland 20810

Dear Mr. Wayne:

I am applying for the position of staff reporter for *The Weekly News.* I saw the job opening listed on the bulletin board at American University.

For the past three years I have worked as a reporter for *The Planet,* the student newspaper at our school. I covered news, wrote feature stories on sports figures and dignitaries, and interviewed politicians, celebrities, and other well-known people who were guest speakers on campus. I contributed two to three articles a week.

Enclosed are my resume and photocopies of three of my feature stories. I would be pleased to meet with you in person. Thank you for your time and your consideration.

Very truly yours,

Klark Kent

Tips for Writing Cover Letters

1. Use 8½-by-11-inch unlined paper. Try to use the same kind of paper you used for your resume. If you can't match it, use good white paper.
2. Be sure the letter is neatly typed and in proper business-letter format, with no errors in grammar or spelling.
3. Address it to a specific person. If you can't find out what the person's name is, write "Dear Sir or Madam" or "To Whom it May Concern."
4. Keep a photocopy or carbon of your letter so you can refer to it if you need to.
5. If you're answering a newspaper ad, clip it and attach it to your copy.

JOB APPLICATIONS

Some entry-level jobs (receptionist, sales clerk), blue-collar jobs (construction worker, factory worker), and professional jobs (government worker, teacher) do not require resumes. Instead, you may have to apply for these jobs by submitting an application. For other jobs you may have to complete an application *and* hand in your resume. Here are some helpful tips for filling out applications.

JOB APPLICATION HINTS

1. Always use blue or black ink to fill out an application. You may also type the application.

2. Be neat and write clearly.
3. If you have a resume, bring it along with you and use phrases from it to fill in the application.
4. Remember to use active verbs when describing your job duties.
5. Answer all questions. If there's a question that doesn't apply to you, write "N/A" (not applicable). That shows the employer you haven't ignored or overlooked the question.
6. Follow the instructions carefully.
7. Use complete names, addresses, telephone numbers (include area codes), and zip codes. It's okay to abbreviate states.
8. Check to make sure words are spelled correctly. If you have a lot of trouble spelling words, take a pocket dictionary with you.
9. When the application form asks what salary you expect, write "negotiable" or "open." If you must give a salary, use a range. For example, if you know that the job starts at $12,000 a year and goes up to $14,000, you can write "$12,000 to $14,000 per year." Do the same for hourly wages (for example, $5.00 to $7.00 per hour).

Take a look at how Terri Berger filled out her job application.

XYZ CORPORATION

APPLICATION FOR EMPLOYMENT

PERSONAL DATA

Date _JUNE 15, 1985_

Name _Berger   Terri   m_ Social Security Number _000-000-0002_
　　　Last　　First　　Middle Initial

Present Address _5736 Broken Lane Belle Meade   N.J. 08502_
　　　　　　　　　　Street　　　　City　　　　　State　　Zip Code

Permanent Address _(same as above)_
　　　　　　　　　Street　　　　City　　　　　State　　Zip Code

No. of years at above address _6_ Phone _(201) 844-2525_

Are you 18 years of age or over? yes _____ no _✓_

EMPLOYMENT

Job applying for _sales training program_ Rate of pay expected _open_ per _____
Date you can start _July 1, 1985_
Have you worked for XYZ before? _NO_ When? _N/A_
What skills or qualifications can you offer XYZ? _I have 2½ years
of sales experience. Have also done inventories and kept
store records_

EDUCATION

Type of School	Name and Address	No. of Years Attended	Graduated Yes　No	Course or Major
Grade or Middle	_Grover Cleveland middle, Belle Meade, N.J._	_4_	_✓_	
High School	_James Madison Belle Meade, N.J._	_4_	_June, 1985_	_Business_
College				
Graduate				
Business/Trade				
Other				

MILITARY SERVICE

U.S. Veteran _N/A_ Branch of Service _____

Date of Active Duty _____ to _____
　　　　　　　　Month　　　Year　　　Month　　　Year

110

WORK EXPERIENCE

Name and Address of Company	Dates	Supervisor	Position	Salary	Reason for Leaving
Thrifty Food Store Belle Meade, NJ Phone (201) 844-1111	Sept 84	Mr. Blake	Sales Clerk	$3.65 hr.	
La Belle Dress Shop Belle Meade, NJ. Phone (201) 844-2222	Jan 83 to Aug. 84	Mrs. Augustine	Sales Clerk	$3.35 hr	Temporary Job
Phone ( )					
Phone ( )					

PERSONAL REFERENCES

Name and Occupation	Address	Phone	Years acquainted
Thomas Blake, store owner.	Thrifty Foods Belle Meade NJ	(201) 844-1111	1½
Jane Augustine, store owner,	La Belle Dress Shop Belle Meade, NJ.	(201) 844-2222	3
John Adams, teacher,	James Madison H.S. Belle Meade, NJ	(201) 844-3434	4

HEALTH INFORMATION

Do you have any physical handicaps or disabilities that would preclude you from performing any specific types of work? __NO__ If so, please describe disability and limitations

SECURITY INFORMATION

Have you been convicted of a felony within the past five years? __No__
If yes, describe _____

I hereby certify that the information I have provided is true. I authorize the XYZ Corporation to investigate my work history and the statements I have made herein.

Terri Berger
Signature

June 15, 1985
Date

111

College and Trade School Applications

Each college, university, and trade school has its own forms. The same hints that apply to job applications also, for the most part, apply to school applications.

1. Review Job Application Hints.
2. Remember, when you're filling out a school application it's helpful to review your Personal Inventory sheet and your resume.
3. You'll need to talk about your strengths on this type of application, so think positively.
4. When answering essay questions, be sure to have someone (teacher, friend, parent) who has good writing and grammar skills read your answers and offer a critique.

PUTTING TOGETHER A PORTFOLIO

You should have a folder (a portfolio) in which to keep copies of your resume and letters of recommendation. Keep all this information in one spot. Then you won't have to go rummaging around the house to find copies of your important papers each time you need them. Take this folder along with you to job or school interviews. That way when the interviewer asks for a resume, a recommendation, or a reference you can respond with "I have it right here."

References and Letters of Recommendation

A reference is *a person* who agrees to testify to your character and ability. When an employer asks for a reference, he or she may call the person you've listed as a reference to check you out. A letter of recommendation is a *written statement* that testifies to your character and ability. If you're applying for a job or to a college, you may be asked for just such a letter or you may be asked to list references on your application. Before you visit a school or go job hunting, talk to several people who know you well—teachers, members of the clergy, employers, or co-workers—and ask each of them to write you a letter of recommendation. It's best to have two or three such letters. Always keep the original letter for your file and make photocopies for handing out or mailing.

Other Tools of the Trade

For some occupational fields you may need to bring samples of your work. For example, if the job you're applying for requires a lot of writing, include in your portfolio articles or papers you've written to show as examples of your work. If your career goal is art-related, collect sketches, photographs, or photos of your work (for example, pictures of sculptures you've done, stage sets you've worked on, costumes you've designed) to put in your portfolio. Tape recordings or video recordings of your performances are great if you're interested in music, drama, television, and other performing arts.

Before going on a job interview, you may want to read Chapter Seven: Building Your Confidence. Self-confidence is one of the keys, not only to getting through a successful job interview, but to getting ahead in life.

7
BUILDING
YOUR
CONFIDENCE

Do you ever start on a new project (learning to play the guitar, writing a short story, getting ready for a job interview) and all of a sudden find yourself stopping short? You can't go on. There's a mountain blocking your way! A mountain? Yes, a mountain. This Everest of anxiety, this obstacle stopping you from getting where you want to go, is made up of nothing more than your own fears, worries, and lack of self-confidence.

What stops you from scaling the mountain? Are you afraid you can't climb that high? Well, you can if you take some time to build your confidence. Self-confidence can be powerful enough to let you soar. The better you feel about yourself, the more your self-esteem will grow—enough to let you conquer your mountain. In this chapter you'll discover some ways to scale even the steepest of peaks. We'll start by calling on some inner resources to help us stretch high enough to make a Mount Everest seem like a little hill.

THE INNER YOU

You've been doing a lot of thinking about your skills, your goals, and some possible careers. But have you really thought about *you:* your feelings, your emotions, the way you look and how you talk about yourself? Let's stop for a minute and try a self-discovery exercise.

Self-Discovery

In your career journal, write "I am" at the top of a new page. Then take two minutes to jot down as many adjectives as you can come up with to describe yourself: your personality, character, behavior, looks, and so forth. Use only one-word adjectives like "patient," "polite," "attractive."

Now read over your list. Which adjectives describe you in a positive way? Which in a negative way? Circle the positive adjectives. Then count how many times you were positive and how many times you were negative in describing yourself. The higher your score, the stronger your belief in your own abilities—in other words, the higher your confidence level.

But if today was a bummer, you may have a lot of negatives. That's because your feelings of self-esteem may change from day to day, situation to situation. For example, you may be the class whiz at math and go into a math test smiling and confident. But suppose you have to play in a tennis match and you spend most of your time on the court hitting the ball into the net? You may not feel all that confident as the day of the tournament approaches.

What can you do to keep your confidence level high, even if you do end up with more net balls than scoring shots? Let's stop and take a closer look at confidence—how you project it to others, how it helps you get what you want out of life, and how it helps you land a job.

Confident People

Picture three people whom you admire and think of as confident. They may be people you know or public figures. Notice the kind of judgments you make about these people and what you base these impressions on. Note how these people look, act, move, dress, behave. Then write down some of these traits. For example, maybe you admire comedian Bill Cosby. Why? Because he's funny and he's poised. He can laugh at his mistakes. What can you learn from the qualities you admire in him? For example, Bill Cosby's ability to laugh at himself shows that he has enough confidence to make others laugh with him. Take a minute to write down a list of people you admire and what you like about them. Set up your page like this:

PEOPLE I ADMIRE   WHY?

Bill Cosby   He can laugh at himself. He's funny.

Now think about people you know who don't seem confident. Get an image of these people in your mind. How do they look, behave, act, talk? For instance, comedian Rodney Dangerfield makes his living playing a man who "don't get no respect." What does his stage character do to look so unsure of himself? Well, he slumps his shoulders, never smiles, and acts as if the world is out to get him. For Rodney Dangerfield, this role is only an act, but many people out there really live this unhappy part. Now make a list of traits of people who lack confidence. Title your page "Traits of People Who Lack Confidence."

Self-Acceptance

Now that you have some clues about what you do and don't admire in a person, let's consider what makes someone feel confident. First of all, what is self-confidence? It's feeling sure of your own skills and abilities. Perhaps you're beginning to feel more confident now that you've discovered your skills. Knowing what you can do helps you feel good about yourself. Being able to say positive things about yourself and being able to accept compliments also raises your level of self-esteem.

On a page in your career journal titled "Compliments," write down three positive statements about yourself. Start each sentence with "I really feel good about . . ."

How did you feel after completing this exercise? If you were feeling comfortable or happy, you've probably accepted your skills and accomplishments. But what if you felt embarrassed or had trouble thinking of good things to say about yourself? This is a very natural feeling. In our society, we've been taught not to brag, but to be modest. And true, nobody likes a braggart—you know, the type who goes around crowing about how wonderful he is. On the other hand, you're not going to take your best friend along on a job interview with you to tell the employer how organized and efficient you are or what terrific mechanical skills you have. So when you're talking to an employer or college or trade school admissions officer, it's important to mention your skills and strengths in a positive way and convince your interviewer that you're the best one to do the job. Here's how Dawn, a high school junior, handled her job interview:

> INTERVIEWER: This job requires good organizational skills. Do you think you can handle it? (*Here's Dawn's cue to point out some of her strengths without being boastful.*)

> DAWN: Yes. Last year I organized the sophomore class committee. We planned dances, trips, and other activities for two hundred students. I also helped plan and organize the class trip to Disneyland. I chartered several buses and made the seating arrangements on them. Later, I got a lot of compliments on how smoothly the day ran.

Compliments

A second step toward building self-esteem is learning to accept compliments from others. When

someone compliments you on the shirt you're wearing, do you answer, "I got this real cheap on sale" or
"This is really old"? Instead of just saying thank you
and accepting the compliment, do you discount
what the other person said by explaining it away? Or
do you feel that you have to pay the compliment
back immediately? When your friend says, "Your
hair looks great," do you feel compelled to say,
"Yours looks great, too," even if your friend's hair
looks as if it's been combed with an eggbeater? On a
job interview this tendency could mean trouble.
Let's take a look at Jennifer's response.

> INTERVIEWER: Your application is so neatly
> prepared. Did you type it yourself?

> JENNIFER: Yes, I did. But I'm afraid it's not all
> that neat. I kept making mistakes and using
> lots of correction tape.

> INTERVIEWER: Oh, well it looked neat to me.

What did Jennifer's response do to the interviewer's image of her? How would you feel if you were
that person? More than likely, the interviewer felt
embarrassed at thinking the paper was neat in the
first place. Second, the interviewer may have seen
her as a confident, organized person (certainly she
had corrected her form neatly). But when Jennifer
said, "I'm afraid it's not all that neat," she sounded
unsure of herself and she insulted the interviewer.
Here's how Jennifer could have handled the situation in a positive way.

> INTERVIEWER: Your application is so neatly
> prepared. Did you type it yourself?

JENNIFER: Yes, I did type it myself. Thank you.

Thank you? Yes, "thank you." That's all Jennifer needed to say. Now Jennifer felt good about accepting the compliment, and she confirmed the interviewer's judgment. More important, Jennifer came across as a very confident young woman.

For the next week, be aware of how you react to compliments. See if you can say thank you without an explanation. You and a friend might even practice giving and accepting compliments.

Another way to check your attitude about accepting pats on the back is to give yourself compliments while looking at your reflection in a mirror. Start with something simple like "I'm a good volleyball player," "I dress well," or "I draw great cartoons." How do you feel? Slightly giggly? Red in the face? Or do you find a smile spreading across your face? Try some more. Compliment yourself on your character, your talents, or your accomplishments. We need to feel good about ourselves and feel comfortable saying and hearing good things about ourselves. These activities help you develop self-esteem and project confidence to friends, family, teachers, employers, and others.

Putdowns: Potholes on the Road to Success

Another way to raise your self-esteem is to stop putting yourself down. We all know our own weaknesses, probably even better than we know our strengths. It's easy to dwell on these weaknesses and to point them out to ourselves and others. How many times, while on your way over the mountain of fear, have you stumbled into one of these potholes? Joe Walker fell into these potholes whenever he worried about his basketball playing. He constantly told himself, "Keith always makes more points than I do. I'm a lousy basketball player. I'm really going to blow it in tonight's game." Suddenly he no longer looked forward to playing. His confidence level sank. He'd "psyched himself down" for a poor performance, and that night he would play badly.

Everybody has a bad day now and then, but in this case, Joe really set himself up for failure. Perhaps if he hadn't spent the day putting himself down, he might have done better. What could Joe have done when he felt himself getting shaky?

Next time, Joe tried thought-stopping. That is, every time he found himself thinking a negative thought, he yelled "Stop"—either to himself or out loud, if he was alone. Immediately, he recognized his self-putdown. Saying "Stop" was a signal to change his negative thought to a positive one.

"Now when I feel shaky, I stop my negative thoughts. Instead, I think about how many shots I've set up in previous games. I think about my contribution and how important my teamwork is in winning points. I even begin to think of new plays," Joe explained. Joe changed his "I'm a rotten player" to "I'm a good team player," and he's no longer worrying about points, but concentrating on helping his teammates. Now he looks forward to games.

When you're good at recognizing and stopping negative thoughts, you can try out another way of being positive—visualizing yourself positively in a situation. According to career expert Howard Figler, "pictures are more powerful than words and can tell you a great deal about what you desire." If every night, Joe took a few minutes to practice playing basketball in his mind—closing his eyes and imagining himself putting the ball through the hoop—his positive pictures would enhance his playing almost as much as actual practice. Sound ridiculous? Well, a study was done of two sets of basketball players—one set that practiced mentally and another that practiced on the court. The surprising results were that the boys who "practiced in pictures" did almost as well as those who actually got out on the court each day. Imagine what would happen if they did both? Next time you find yourself having doubts about what you can do, try visualizing what you could do.

THE OUTER YOU

How can you project your positive feelings and your assets to other people, particularly employers, recruiters, and admissions officers? You can begin by becoming aware of how you convey messages through your facial expressions, your eyes, and the way you walk, talk, and move. Let's take a look at this more closely.

Body Language

The picture or image you present to the world (in school or on the job or job hunt) is projected through your body language, speech, movement, and dress.

You've heard the old expression, "You can't judge a book by its cover." However, it's often the book's jacket or title that makes you want to pick it up and open it. It may seem unfair, but we do make judgments about people during the first few minutes after we meet them. We decide we like them or we don't; we decide they're lazy or ambitious; we decide they're competent or disorganized. How do we pick up these clues?

Jennifer slinks into the office, chewing gum and wearing a T-shirt and jeans. Immediately, she sends negative signals to Ms. Johnson, the interviewer, which makes Ms. Johnson wonder how suitable Jennifer will be as a salesclerk in her dress shop. With her slumped shoulders and lack of eye contact, Jennifer has "loser" written all over her.

A little later in the day, Cathy comes in to be interviewed for the same position. Dressed in a skirt and blouse, with her hair attractively combed, Cathy makes a confident first impression. From her firm handshake to her friendly smile, Cathy clearly comes across as a winner.

What made the difference? At first glance, you might think it was the way they were dressed. And it's true that the way we dress says a lot about how we feel about ourselves and our attitude toward others. For example, by wearing jeans—a totally inappropriate outfit—Jennifer came across as not thinking the job was worth getting dressed up for. Cathy, on the other hand, showed she cared about how she looked and how others felt about her by paying careful attention to her grooming.

Equally or maybe even more important was the way each young woman carried herself. Body language—the way you move, hold your body (posture), and gesture—sends messages to other people. Jennifer's slumped shoulders, wandering gaze, and gum chewing clue others into her awkwardness. So uncomfortable is she with herself that she may make others feel slightly fidgety, too. When Cathy enters with a firm stride and a smile, she exudes positive energy. Who would you rather be around? Who would you hire? If your goal is to keep customers flocking in, you'll choose Cathy. But if you're bent on bankruptcy, Jennifer is your best bet.

Before these girls have even begun to talk, their appearance and body language have said reams about them. Nonverbal cues let other people see how we feel about ourselves and the situation we encounter. As a matter of fact, experts who've studied body language have concluded that most of the messages we send to people are conveyed through our body language, not the words we say. In answer to the question, "What kind of job do you want?" picture what a shrug of the shoulders says to the interviewer. This one little motion probably suggests "I haven't given much thought about this," and even more damaging than that, it projects a couldn't-care-less attitude.

The Eyes Have It

Another important way we communicate is through our eyes. Shakespeare called eyes "the windows of the soul." You can tell a lot about people by the way they use their eyes. For example, have you ever been to a party and stopped to chat with a friend? Suddenly, even though your friend is carrying on a conversation with you, you get the feeling he's not really there. What gave you that feeling? Chances are it's the fact that his eyes are not focused on you but seem to be wandering around the room as you're talking. You probably have the feeling your friend is looking for someone else to talk to and that's he's only killing time chatting with you.

Keeping eye contact, looking into an individual's eyes as you speak, lets the other person know that you think he's important. He knows you're listening to him, and it indicates that you are serious about what you're saying. Lack of eye contact, on the other hand, can be devastating on a job interview. Your interviewer, when met with a pair of wandering eyes, would probably think that you'd rather be outside playing ball or at home reading a book.

The other extreme, staring the interviewer down until she squirms in her seat, certainly won't get you the job either. Try to strike a balance. Most likely if you feel comfortable, the person you're talking to will feel relaxed, too.

About Faces

The expression we wear on our faces is another important nonverbal cue. How can you tell if someone's happy, sad, angry, or serious? Usually all you have to do is look at that person's face. A smile, a tear, a frown, a wrinkled brow reflect the person's mood. Our faces are fairly accurate mirrors of what's going on inside us. However, in stressful situations like interviewing for a job or applying for a business loan, we want to make a good impression. Because we're trying so hard, we plaster smiles on our faces, creating false fronts. Smiling is good, but make sure it matches your message.

Peter's smile was certainly welcome when he met Ms. Adams, the college recruiter. But as the meeting proceeded, his unnatural grinning, even when asked serious questions—like "What are your plans for the future?"—gave Ms. Adams a wrong impression. Peter apeared to be not taking the situation seriously. Facial expressions need to match what you're talking about. If it's a serious conversation, be serious. If it's a humorous situation, go ahead and smile. However, when the discussion turns to matters like responsibility and judgment, a more thoughtful expression is appropriate. In other words, don't be false. Try to keep your facial expressions natural. You don't have to keep smiling like a Miss or Mr. America contestant. (Anyhow, the only way to maintain this grinning, is to do what these contestants do—smear petroleum jelly on their teeth. This is hardly fitting for a job interview and it probably doesn't taste very good either.)

Sound Off

Bill has an interview for a job at McDonald's. Dressed in slacks and a shirt, he walks in and shakes hands with the manager. So far, with his confident stride, neat appearance, and firm handshake he's made a great impression. Then he opens his mouth.

"Hi, I'm Bill mzmzmzmz,"he mumbles.

"Pardon me?" says the manager.

"I'm Bill mzmzmzmz," he mumbles again.

"Bill what?" asks the manager as he shakes his head in dismay.

If Bill had spoken clearly, his tone of voice would have supported the fine impression he made as he walked in. But mumbling indicated to the manager

Bill's lack of confidence. Right away the manager decided that Bill's voice was not a good one for dealing with customers. Bill struck out before he got up to bat. The rest of the interview didn't matter.

How you speak says quite a bit about you. A squeaky little voice squeals "I'm a little mousy person" to anyone listening. Certainly an employer isn't going to want that voice to answer the company telephone. A breathy, Bo Derek voice, might earn you a role in a remake of the movie "10," but this whispery tone of voice wouldn't get you a shot at a job in a high-technology firm.

On the other hand, a trumpeting voice is great for yelling at the umpire at baseball games, but not for a job in banking. Imagine how the customers would cringe as you boomed out the current balance of their savings accounts for all to hear. You don't want to come across as "poor little me" or "I know it all." Or even worse, a whiner—one of those nerve-janglers who cry for what they want. A moderate voice with good tone and clear enunciation reflects confidence and is the kind of voice most people enjoy listening to.

To test what you sound like, try talking into a tape recorder. If you're stumped for something to say, answer a question like "What do you like doing best?" Play back your response. If you've never heard your voice on tape, you probably won't believe it's you. (We all sound a bit different to ourselves.) Listen to see if you speak clearly, if you're speaking too loud or too low, and how you're coming across to others. Then try to analyze your voice.

You may also want to check with a friend or family member to find out how you sound to them. Probably with a few minor adjustments and some practice you can sound great. Maybe you're one who doesn't need any help in this area at all. But if you do want help, check out speech courses at your local Y or community college.

Putting this all together—speaking clearly and effectively, using body language to project a positive image, and making eye contact—may seem like too much to concentrate on and may even seem contrived. But being aware of how you look, sound, and move, combined with a bit of practice will help you eliminate some of the shakiness. In time, these techniques will come naturally and at the right moment. And as a bonus, looking confident on the outside will boost your self-esteem.

UNDERMINERS OF CONFIDENCE

But what about those times when you're facing a new and scary situation—something big and seemingly insurmountable? That's when your self-esteem could take a nose dive. All the "I can'ts," or "I should haves" stop you. "I should have been better prepared for the interview," you tell yourself. "I can't face another employer," you wail.

Sometimes, when you face a new situation, that old mountain of fear may rise up in front of you once more. Now you have to deal with your old anxieties all over again. What do you do? You can sit down and cry. You can go back home and hide. Or you can look at the mountain of fear as a challenge and figure out a plan to conquer it.

Fear of Failure

Many times the mountain of fear is very real—a

mammoth obstacle that may require some steady footwork to climb over the summit. For example, to get into most colleges you will have to take a standardized test, the SAT. If your confidence level is low, your fears may make that obstacle (the test) seem impossible to handle so that your fear becomes not just Mount Everest but all the rest of the Himalayas, too.

Sometimes you're so worried about failing that you're afraid to take risks. Your fears and anxieties cause you to make a poor decision or no decision at all. You might decide the test is impossible and therefore spend more time worrying about it than studying for it. Or you might just decide that you won't take the exam, eliminating college as a career choice, when in fact going to college is something you want to do. In either case, in your mind, the mountain has become insurmountable.

Conquering the Mountain

But maybe you're more realistic. You'll take a good look at that mountain before you decide to forgo the climb. There may be ways to conquer it if you want to get over to the other side badly enough. You could take a preparatory course on the SAT. You could brush up on your math, if you're not good with numbers. In other words, having a plan can minimize your risks. It's the difference between having a road map to your destination and having to plod along without map or compass to help you figure out the direction.

You can also take little steps to go over the mountain. It's much easier than trying to make one huge leap. So try breaking down what you have to do into small steps. (Look back at Chapter Three and see how to break a goal down into steps.) Then the problem becomes much more manageable.

Self-image is very important in helping you conquer your fears, too. You first need to get rid of all those "I can'ts," especially before they turn into "I won't because I'm afraid." Remember Joe Walker whose anxieties about his playing undermined his basketball game? When he began to thought-stop and then visualize himself in a positive way, he could go on and play the game. Thought-stopping and visualization can help you in new situations. "Seeing" yourself on the other side is the first step in getting over there.

For example, picture yourself sitting down with a math book and reviewing what you already know. Then picture yourself taking the SAT and finally sitting in college as a student. Then every time one of those "I can'ts" rears its ugly head, you can replace it with a positive thought—an affirmation. "I can't possibly pass the test" becomes an "I'm going to do the best I can on the test." In other words, you are making an "I can't" into an "I can." For instance, "I can't get a job because I don't have experience" could be changed into "I'm doing volunteer work so that I will have experience to get a job." You're changing an "I can't" to an "I will." In doing that, you find a solution to a problem and give your self-esteem a boost at the same time.

When making affirmations, be sure they're realistic. Don't set yourself up for failure. For example, it wouldn't be such a great idea to tell yourself you're going to get straight A's, if you're pulling a C average and there are only two weeks left till the end of the marking period. You'll only end up frustrated and angry. Instead, make a reasonable affirmation like this: "I'll work hard for the rest of the semester and do my best on the final exam." Maybe next term you can try for some A's.

Now open your career notebook and write a few affirmations about yourself. Think about a new situation that you're facing—job, school, or volunteer work, for example. What fears immediately come to your mind? You may want to jot these fears down on a page in your career notebook set up like this:

NEW SITUATION	FEARS	AFFIRMATIONS
Finding a job	Not enough experience	I am doing volunteer work so that I will have enough experience to get the job.

Developing a plan, visualizing yourself in a positive way, and making positive statements about yourself will give you the self-esteem necessary to conquer your mountain, no matter how large or how small your fears. Remember, you can't build confidence overnight. You need to reinforce your self-esteem constantly by acknowledging your skills and your strengths, accepting compliments from others, and visualizing yourself positively in various situations. Eleanor Roosevelt once said, "No one can make you feel inferior without your consent." Who you are and what you are is up to you—no one else. When you're feeling good about yourself, you project this to other people and they—your family, friends, teachers, employers—all feel good about you, too.

Since you've just worked on building confidence, try repeating the "I am" exercise that you did at the beginning of the chapter. Once more, title a page "I am" and take two minutes to write down as many adjectives as you can come up with to describe yourself: your personality, character, behavior, looks, and so forth. Use one-word adjectives.

See how easy it is to feel good about yourself? Now you're ready to go out and face the world.

8
GOING ON
JOB
INTERVIEWS

It's time to take all you've learned about yourself and the world of work and head out into the job arena. Now all you need is a job interview. The big question is how do you go about getting one?

SEEKING OUT JOB INTERVIEWS

Newspapers

The most obvious place to look when you want a job is the want ads in local newspapers. This is a good place to begin searching because it gives you an idea what kinds of jobs are available and what employers are looking for. However, don't count on getting a job this way. According to the career expert Richard Bolles, only about 25 percent of all jobs are advertised through want ads. The other 75 percent are filled by word of mouth, through employment agencies, or in many cases, by someone the employer already has in mind. However, answering ads gives you a chance to find out if your resume sparks an employer's interest. You have nothing to lose by trying this method, but don't make it your only choice. It could lead to a job interview, if you know how to use a want ad effectively.

Let's take a closer look at a want ad.

General Office Clerk

High-tech firm has entry level position for individual to process daily sales reports. Must have ability to use 10-key adding machine and communicate effectively over the phone. $4/hour. Send resumes to Mr. Ultra, Two-Bit Systems, Station Square, Pittsburgh, PA. 15225.

TIPS ON USING THE WANT ADS

1. Read each want ad carefully. Look for the job title.
2. Circle any skills the job requires.
3. Notice if the ad names a person or company or just a box number. If a company's name is on the want ad, the

employer is more likely to respond because the company's reputation is on the line. If you do answer a box number, don't hold your breath while waiting for an answer. You may never hear from the person who placed the ad.

4. If the ad lists a job you're really interested in, write a letter to accompany your resume (see Chapter Six). Don't forget to highlight the skills you have that match those in the want ad.

5. Don't sit around waiting for a response. Keep looking. There's a lot of truth in the old saying "Don't put all your eggs in one basket."

State Employment and Training Centers

You can register for jobs at your state employment office. In addition to filling out forms and talking briefly with a counselor, you can use the microfiche or files, which list some of the job openings in your area. This service agency tends to specialize in blue-collar jobs. However, other types of work may also be available. It's worth a try. Remember, the more contacts you make, the greater your chances of finding a job. Also, the more people you talk to, the more relaxed you become at interviewing.

Junior or Senior High School Guidance Offices or College Career Development Offices

If you're lucky enough to have a school guidance department that helps with job placement, schedule an appointment with an adviser. Or go to your local community college career center and see what help the counselors there can give you. Often you can get help with your resume and look up information about local employers. Many times there will be a bulletin board with job listings on it as well.

Employment Agencies

You might also consider registering with a job placement or employment agency. This is fine if you know just what kind of job you're after and aren't willing to sell yourself short. Since some agencies may try to place you in a job just because it's available and you are, too, you must know exactly what you want to do, so you don't end up in a job delivering newspapers when you really want to be writing for the sports section.

Sometimes you may want to work so badly that you'll be tempted to grab the first job you're offered. Taking any job may seem appealing in order to end the long looking process, but remember all of the hours you've already invested in planning and preparing for your future. Don't go out job hunting with an I'll-take-anything attitude. Sally was looking forward to a career in public relations. She had good communication skills and could type. The recruiter at the agency suggested a position as administrative aide, filing and typing letters in the accounting department of a hospital. Sally asked herself, How could this job help me with my career? When she thought about this, she realized that while she had the qualifications to take the hospital job, this was not a position that would give her experience in public relations.

If you do decide to go to an employment agency, keep the following suggestions in mind:

1. Read the contract carefully. Contracts differ from agency to agency.
2. Beware of contracts that tie you down to the job for longer than you would like. For example, when the employment agency found a job for Sally, she was asked to sign a contract requiring her to stay with the company for two years. What if Sally really didn't like the job? Two years would seem like forever.
3. Be sure the job is what you're looking for.
4. Find out who's paying the fee, you or the company. Before you consider paying a fee to get a job, try all other possibilities.

Resumes

Many job seekers print hundreds of resumes and send them out to anyone and everyone. Generally all this does is make a lot of printing companies richer. A resume can be an effective tool in getting a job when it's accompanied by a good cover letter and sent to the right company. You've got to do some research first, though, just as you did on those information interviews. Find out the companies you'd like to work for and the companies that have the kind of job you'd like to do. Then send your resume and cover letter to the person who can hire you—not to the personnel office. If you're going to use this method of job hunting, go back and review Chapter Six.

Networking

What other possibilities are there for seeking out job interviews? Richard Bolles says that the best way to get a job is through people you know. So let all your friends and family know you're looking. They, too, can keep their ears open for job vacancies. John told everyone he knew that he was looking for a job as a garage mechanic. One of his brother's friends worked at a local gas station. When he heard of an upcoming opening at the station, he mentioned it to John. John immediately called the station and got an early interview along with a recommendation from his brother's friend—which put him one step ahead of the want ad watchers. He eventually got the job. This is a form of networking—using your contacts to help you.

Joining an organization associated with the kind of job you want to do is another form of networking. For example, Gail wanted to work in a library, so she decided to look up the local chapter of the library association and attend a meeting. Here she met many people who worked in the field. She told several of them that she was looking for a job. A couple of people took copies of her resume. She even got the names and numbers of a few people to call for an interview.

Information Interviews

Don't forget all those information interviews you've gone on. Remember that list you made of people you visited? Take it out and let all those people know you're job hunting. They've already had a good look at you, so you'll have an advantage over others who are just starting to send in resumes. Employers prefer to hire someone they know rather than a complete stranger. In calling people on that list, you may find they don't have any jobs available. However, they can pass on your name and resume to someone who is hiring or perhaps they will give you some other leads to call.

Making Your Own Job Lead—Doing Detective Work

Sometimes it helps to play Sherlock Holmes and track down a job lead. You may have to do some fancy footwork to get in the door. Be creative. How might you find out about job leads in your field?

If Sandy wanted a job in construction he might look in the real estate section of the newspaper and see where new homes are going up. Then he could go to the site and ask about jobs. Barbara wanted a job as a computer data entry typist in a high-technology firm. Where would be the most likely place to find a job? Reasoning that new companies would be needing personnel, she visited her local government's Office for Economic Development and asked what new high-tech firms were moving into her area. She got the names and addresses of the new companies and wrote them letters in advance, telling them about her qualifications, and including a copy of her resume. These companies now had someone they could call on when they moved into the area. Barbara had a foot in the door. She could also follow up her lead by calling on each company.

Asking questions is a good way to begin playing detective. Start with yourself. Answer the following questions in your journal on a page labeled "Interview Ideas."

1. What field do you want to work in?
2. What type of company or organization would you like to work for—medical, high tech, auto, advertising, arts, sales?
3. What could you do for that type of company or organization?
4. How can you find out the names of specific organizations or companies?

After answering these questions, you might do just as you did in information interviewing: ask others for names of companies; look in professional journals, telephone directories, and magazines; read newspaper ads; go to the chamber of commerce and/or visit a career development center.

If you're a sharp job hunter, you'll maximize your chances by using a combination of all these methods to get a job interview. After all, the more people you know, the better your chances of getting a job.

WAYS TO PREPARE FOR THE JOB INTERVIEW

Your legwork has finally paid off. At last you've been successful in lining up a job interview. Don't let panic set in. Instead, take some small steps to get ready for the big day.

Presenting Your Skills

Go back over your Skills chart and note which of your skills match those in the job description. Now be prepared to talk about those skills in a positive way. One way to do this is to pick out two or three accomplishments from your skills list and prepare to describe them to the interviewer.

Turning Disadvantages into Advantages

Be ready to answer questions about your inexperience. If you haven't had much work experience, think about your accomplishments in school, social areas, and part-time jobs like baby-sitting or lawn mowing. For example, if the job requires leadership skill, point out that you've been president of your computer club, if you've held that office. If the employer asks about your mathematical skills, you may want to explain that you developed a budget and are keeping the financial records for the club this year, if you've done that.

Know your weaknesses as well as your strengths. Very often interviewers will ask you to point to a weakness. (Keep in mind, they're not talking about weaknesses like pigging out at the campus cafeteria.) Give this one some thought ahead of time because this question can put you at a disadvantage. For instance, how will you make a trait like impatience work for you rather than against you? Well, you could look at the positive side of that weakness. For example, you could say, "I'm impatient and I get things done quickly." Or if you're the opposite, a bit slow, you could turn that around by saying, "I work slowly, and I do a thorough job." Take out your notebook and set up a page like this and then fill in the blanks:

WEAKNESS	TURNAROUNDS
1. I am _____ and	I _____.
2. I am _____ and	I _____.

This is another kind of affirmation. Once you start turning a weakness into a strength, it will begin to work for you rather than against you.

Doing Your Homework

Find out as much as you can about the employer, company, or organization before your interview. What is the exact address and how do you get there? You may have to call for directions. Make sure you find out how to pronounce and spell the name of the interviewer.

Try to get a job description ahead of time. Call and see if the secretary will mail you one. If it's a small business, they probably won't have a written statement, but perhaps they'd be willing to describe the job duties over the phone.

If it's a big company, try to read up on it. You can request an annual report or in-house publications. Some of this information may be available in your library. Check with the reference librarian there.

Questions the Interviewer May Ask You

The questions below are often asked on job interviews. Practice answering them so you'll be well prepared for the interview.

1. Tell me about yourself. (*Hint:* This is not a license to give a detailed autobiography starting with the hospital you were born in. Here's where you talk

about skills and accomplishments.
Linda, who was applying for a summer
job teaching arts and crafts to children,
answered this way: "I've always been
interested in art. Throughout high school
I took lessons, drew funny sketches for
the yearbook, and painted posters for
school events.)

2. Do you know anything about our
   organization?
3. What are your five-year goals?
4. What are your strengths?
5. What are your weaknesses?
6. Why do you want to work for our
   company?
7. Do you think you have enough
   experience?
8. What kind of salary do you expect?
9. Are you willing to travel?
10. In this job, you might have to perform
    tasks that you don't like doing. How do
    you feel about that? (For example, you
    may answer this way: "I'm not too fond
    of filing, but if some filing has to be done
    for better organization, that's okay.")
11. What do you like doing best?
12. What are your hobbies?
13. Do you belong to any organizations?
14. What jobs have you held in the past?
15. Do you prefer working with others or by
    yourself?
16. Can you get recommendations or letters
    of reference?
17. Do you have any questions?

Questions for You to Ask the Interviewer

You may have some questions for the interviewer at the end of your talk. You may need information before considering this job or comparing it to another. Also, asking about the company takes the focus off you and gives the interviewer a chance to talk. Well-thought-out and appropriate questions show you're interested in the company and that you're serious about your job search.

1. What's an average workday like here?
2. What are the hours?
3. What are the opportunities for advancement with your company?
4. What is the salary for this job? (Don't lead off with this question.)
5. What benefits do you offer your employees? (For example, sick leave, vacation, insurance. Ask this question last.)

It's all right, even important, to ask questions about salary and benefits because you need this information. Leaving these questions until last shows that they're not your only concern.

Perhaps you've thought of some other questions that pertain to your specific job interview. Take a moment to list them in your notebook.

Tips to Remember for a Job Interview

1. Practice for the interview—posture, voice, handshake.
2. Pick out appropriate clothing.
3. Bring your portfolio containing your resume, letters of reference, sketches, photos, and other materials. Also be sure to have a pad, pencil, and your list of questions.
4. Be on time.
5. Be courteous to other office workers— receptionist, secretary, and so forth.
6. Shake hands firmly with the interviewer.
7. Try some icebreakers to get the conversation rolling. Some good starters are the weather, pictures on the wall, and your trip to the company office. Don't go overboard, though.
8. Make eye contact during the interview.
9. Avoid fidgeting and other nervous gestures. Place your hands quietly in your lap if you're prone to the jitters. No chewing gum. Another trap to avoid is playing with paper clips, pencils, or anything on the interviewer's desk. Don't read memos or mail, either.
10. When the interview is over, thank the interviewer for his or her consideration and politely ask, "When can I expect to hear from you?"

Remember, once you've gotten past the icebreakers like talking about the weather, let the interviewer ask the questions. Be sure to answer with enthusiasm and maintain eye contact. You've already prepared your answers, and if your mind should go blank, you can always look down at your resume to refresh your memory. Don't forget to ask the questions you've prepared about the company. Find a convenient time toward the end of the interview to ask them. (For additional suggestions, review Chapter Four and Chapter Seven.)

Following Up

If your interview went well and your interviewer spent a lot of time with you, you might send a thank-you note. This is a courteous gesture, and it will keep you in the interviewer's mind. Here's the note Barbara wrote to Two-Bit Systems:

April 5, 19—

Mr. Hy Ultra
Vice-President
Two-Bit Systems
Station Square
Pittsburgh, PA 15225

Dear Mr. Ultra:

Thank you for the interview on Tuesday. I really
enjoyed talking to you about the data entry job and
learning about the new systems Two-Bit is working
on. It sounds like a challenging and exciting job.

If you need any more information about my
experience, please call me at 844-2525.

Sincerely,

Barbara Blank

Waiting

If you haven't heard about the job within the time your interviewer indicated, wait a few days and then call again. You might do what Gail did.

GAIL: Hi, this is Gail Jones. You interviewed me for the library aide's job three weeks ago. I'm calling to see if any decision has been made about hiring.

INTERVIEWER: We've been bogged down in work here, and we haven't made a decision yet. We expect to make one within the next week.

GAIL: Is there any other information I can give you that might help?

INTERVIEWER: No. I think we have enough information now, but thanks for asking.

GAIL: Thank you very much. I look forward to hearing from you soon.

CLOSED DOORS

If you don't get the job, it's okay to call and find out why. Here's what Gail could say if she didn't get the job:

GAIL: Can you give me any information that would help me on my next job interview? Maybe you can tell me why I didn't get the job. Knowing why would help me prepare for future interviews.

INTERVIEWER: Well, we thought you had good communication skills but not enough experience working with people.

GAIL: Thank you. That's very helpful for me to know.

Gail can then weigh this information. Is it just that this job in particular didn't work out, or has she heard this same comment from several employers? If so, maybe she needs to start looking for an entry-level job. Or maybe she should get more experience through volunteer work while she's job hunting. She might volunteer at the library or offer to take library book carts around to bedridden patients at a hospital.

Dealing with Rejection

Nobody likes being turned down. It's hard not to take rejection personally. When you're turned down for a job, you may feel shaky and insecure. It may help to remember that the employer doesn't really know you and is not rejecting you personally. It could be that someone came along who had more experience or was better suited to the job. Think about times you've had to make a choice. Maybe you've been in a store and can't decide which of two shirts to buy. After some thought, you finally decide on one. Perhaps it goes better with a pair of slacks you have or it may fit more comfortably. It doesn't mean the other shirt isn't good, only that the one you've chosen is better for you. Well, it's the same way with a job sometimes. The interviewer has to make a choice, and it's not always easy. Only one person can get the job, and many will be turned down.

Or maybe the interview didn't go well. See what you can learn from this experience and what you need to improve. After each appointment fill out an Interview Evaluation Chart. Set one up in your notebook like this.

INTERVIEW EVALUATION CHART

Date	Company Interviewer Address Telephone	What I handled well	What needs improvement
7/20	Madras Co. John Doe 1 Checker Sq. St. Louis, MO 63141 641-2112	talking about my skills	eye contact handshake

You may find you will need to go back and practice interviewing with a friend to patch up your weak spots. Keep in mind, too, that finding a job is a full-time job. Getting a job takes a lot of resourcefulness, hard work, and stick-to-itiveness. In many cases, it also takes a long time; it can take from six to eight months of interviewing, or even longer.

If you don't get the jobs you've interviewed for, it's okay to feel a bit sad—that's natural. Try not to wallow in rejection, though; instead, let yourself bounce back quickly. Buy yourself an ice cream soda or smash around a tennis ball to get rid of your frustration. Then get out and hit the road again, trying a new route. As you continue to go on interviews, you'll find that you'll be more relaxed and effective, especially if you take a few minutes after each appointment to write down your impressions in your journal.

 # CONCLUSION: MOVING ON

You've just reached the last step in this journey of self-discovery and career exploration. With your finished career plan, you've edged closer to that ideal day you envisioned ten years into the future. Flipping back through your career journal's pages, you'll find a record of who you are (skills, priorities, goals, self-esteem) and of some career choices you've made (researching careers, information interviewing, entrepreneurship). In addition, you'll have learned techniques to use to land a job, make decisions, and set up your own business.

Before you close your career journal, take a moment to pull together a short summary of your plan.

This summary, your Career Profile, will be a handy guide to head you in the right direction, not with wild leaps but with thoughtful moves.

YOUR CAREER PROFILE

Title a new page in your notebook "My Career Profile." Then copy the chart below and fill it in, looking back over the exercises you've completed in your notebook.

MY CAREER PROFILE

Date _____

Main Skill Areas
[See "My Skills" exercise.]

1. _____
2. _____

Used with:
[Check appropriate answer(s).]
   Data _____
   People _____
   Things _____

Personal Strengths
[Listed in your "I Am" exercises.]

1. _____
2. _____
3. _____

Life Priorities

1. _____
2. _____
3. _____

Work Priorities

1. _____
2. _____
3. _____

Long-Range Goals

1. _____
2. _____
3. _____

Medium-Range Goals

1. _____
2. _____
3. _____

Short-Range Goals

1. _____
2. _____
3. _____

Career Interests
[See "Jobs to Explore."]

1. _____
2. _____
3. _____

Few of us stand still, and you'll find that as you grow and mature, so will your profile. Over the next few years, as you finish school, go out into the job market, or go on to further education, you can go back and update your plan. You can use this book and the exercises in it over and over again to help you find a new job or make a career change and move on.

# BIBLIOGRAPHY

Bolles, Richard N. *What Color Is Your Parachute?* Berkeley, Calif.: Ten Speed Press, 1985.

Career World (magazine).

Dictionary of Occupational Titles. Washington, D.C.: U.S. Department of Labor, Employment and Training Administration, 1977. Also see Supplements.

Figler, Howard. *The Complete Job-Search Handbook.* New York: Holt, Rinehart & Winston, 1979.

Guide for Occupational Exploration. Washington, D.C.: U.S. Department of Labor, Employment and Training Administration, 1984.

Irish, Richard. *Go Hire Yourself an Employer.* New York: Anchor Books, 1978.

Jackson, Tom, and Davidyne Mayleas. *The Hidden Job Market for the 80's.* New York: Times Books, 1981.

Kingstone, Brett M. *The Student Entrepreneur's Guide.* Berkeley, Calif.: Ten Speed Press, 1983.

Lakein, Alan. *How to Get Control of Your Time and Your Life.* New York: New American Library, 1973.

Lathrop, Richard. *Who's Hiring Who.* Berkeley, Calif.: Ten Speed Press, 1977.

Occupational Outlook Handbook. Washington, D.C.: U.S. Department of Labor, Employment and Training Administration, 1984–85.

Scholz, Nelle Tumlin et al. *How To Decide: A Workbook for Women.* New York: Avon Books, 1978.

Winefordner, David W., et al. *Worker Trait Group Guide.* Bloomington, Ill.: McKnight, 1978.

INDEX

159

ABOUT THE AUTHORS

Carolyn Males is a free-lance writer whose articles on careers, mental health, social issues, and travel and recreation have apeared in national magazines including *READER'S DIGEST, TRAVEL/HOLIDAY, THE SATURDAY EVENING POST, COSMOPOLI-TAN, WRITER'S DIGEST,* and *PARADE.* She has also worked as a newspaper reporter, taught writing courses and seminars at local colleges, and has co-authored several novels.

Ms. Males is a former director of Womanscope (now Careerscope), a career counseling and job information center. In addition, she has given career courses and job-finding workshops for universities and colleges, the Girl Scouts of America, high schools, public service employee programs, professional and community organizations, and hospitals. Ms. Males holds an M.A. from the University of Maryland.

Roberta Feigen is Testing and Assessment Specialist at Technical Occupations Employment Group in Rockville, Maryland, where she evaluates the skills, abilities, and work experience of applicants interested in high tech career opportunities. She also gives career counseling to young adults making their first career decisions. As a career development consultant, Ms. Feigen has worked with individual clients, businesses, community organizations, and colleges and has designed and facilitated career education and entrepreneurial education workshops for high school students.

Ms. Feigen has also served as Director of Careerscope, a career counseling and job information center. Prior to this, she taught in public schools in New York City and Maryland. Ms. Feigen earned her B.A. in education at Brooklyn College and her M.A. from Loyola College in Maryland. She is also a wife, homemaker, and mother of two young adults.